TEAM PLAY

STRATEGIES FOR SUCCESSFUL PEOPLE MANAGEMENT

Shirley McKinnon

For my mum, who always understood

First published 1998

National Library of Australia
Cataloguing-in-Publication data:
McKinnon, Shirley.
Team play: strategies for successful people management.

This edition: Createspace 2012

ISBN-13: 978-1480143586

ISBN-10: 1480143588

Front cover photograph by Fisher Photography
Cartoons by Janet Wolf

Typeset by *Ding!* Author Services

CONTENTS

4 DO THEY FEEL LISTENED TO? - 51

5 TRIGGERING OTHER PEOPLE - 69

6 THE PUZZLE OF LOW SELF-ESTEEM - 83

PROLOGUE

David Brownston stared blindly out of the train window and wondered what he was doing wrong. He'd been in the job for six months now, and with all his experience of dealing with people, he should have his team really pumping. They were going reasonably well, but...

The uncomfortable part of it was that he suspected he was having very little influence on them. Some months were good, others were mediocre. Sometimes, he could see a rep was going to miss budget and couldn't seem to do a thing about it. Other times, it came as a complete surprise to both him and the rep. And, if he was honest with himself, with or without his help, they picked themselves up, put in the effort and hours needed, and exceeded beyond all expectations the following month. So why couldn't he get them doing that every month?

He was the sales manager of a dedicated team that was exceeding budget. But too often they struggled in last-minute bursts of desperation. And while the team was jubilant that they had done it again, David knew that there had to be a better way.

When he took this job, he had pictured a slow, solid building of client bases for his people and had worked on building their skills and motivation. But there were days when their contempt for him was obvious, weeks when he couldn't get one of them to take him out with them on client meetings. He let his mind linger on them individually, itemising the issues he saw they had.

Problems with the sales team

There was Nicole, vivacious and bubbly. Nicole was a night-mare when it came to paperwork. Being disorganised seemed as natural as breathing to her. She created chaos in the office, but her clients loved her. She was bright and fun to have around and most months she did well. Occasionally, she soared and wrote the kind of figures that David knew she was capable of achieving every month. But every time she hit the big figures, some personal drama would happen and take her focus off her work. There would be a new man in her life, or an ex-boyfriend would reappear, or her sister would have trouble with her husband and Nicole would be there to support her, or one of the other reps would have a problem and Nicole would somehow become involved. The following month she would be struggling to make budget.

Then there was Sonia. Sonia had a heart of gold. She had years of experience in the industry and she made budget every month — just. It never worried her, though. If she had a great start to her month, she would spend the rest of the month catching up with her old clients over lunch and drinks, and wouldn't sell another thing till the end of the month. She would make budget again — just. She didn't seem to care. It drove David nuts, and he couldn't find a way to motivate her. He'd tried incentives, bonuses, vouchers, free dinners, all kinds of things that he had been told were meant to motivate, and she just smiled and made budget again. Just.

Hamid was a quiet guy, a little distant but very professional. If you asked Hamid to do something, you knew it was going to get done. He would go to the ends of the earth for his clients and they had huge respect for him. The problem was that Hamid took a long time to build a relationship with a client. He was a little distant, not really a warm person, and it always took three to four visits before he made a sale. And it seemed he always had to resell the client. David didn't know how to teach Hamid to make relationships quickly with clients because he himself did it instinctively. Hamid made budget most months, too, but it was hard slog. Even though he was slowly building his client base, it was no easier for him to go back and get repeat sales. And it only took the loss of one client to set him back several months. The truth was that Hamid was getting as frustrated as David was with his performance and David was worried that he was going to lose him. Hamid was very slowly building to become a solid performer, but David didn't know how to get him to the next level. And he needed to get there, fast.

Con was everybody's friend. He was a big softy. His relation-ships with his clients were strong and long-lasting. In fact, Con went too far for his clients, he tended to over-promise and that often resulted in under-delivering. He quite simply couldn't say no to a client. And while he would forgive his clients anything, he was very hard on himself and those around him. David had heard mutterings from Con's clerical assistant. She had spat the dummy one day and maintained that he would never speak to her that way if she was a client. David knew that Con was too soft with his clients and accepted their excuses as real. He knew that Con could double his figures if he would get just a little firmer, but nothing he said seemed to make any difference. They had had a couple of talks and Con had seemed to listen and agree with him, but nothing had changed. David couldn't seem to make an impact on him or change the way he did things.

Last, but not least, there was Gina. Gina was every sales manager's dream. She was totally focused, she had goals she and her husband had set together, and she was determined to succeed. She was professional, organised, good with internal staff and excellent with clients. Most months she was twenty per cent above budget. She loved her job and, to top it all off, she had a stable relationship with her partner. Only a sales manager would know the value of that, thought David to himself. He had begun to wonder if there were any good relationships left out there. It seemed to him that every person in his department took turns each month to have a personal drama. Gina didn't. Well, at least, if she did she kept it to herself until she had solved it. She was a total professional. And that was going to leave him with a problem, too. David knew that it was only a matter of time until either the company promoted her into a management position or she moved elsewhere for promotion. It would be great for her, but he would lose the only person he seemed to be able to influence in the department. Gina had great systems that she used to keep her on track. He had used them several times as an example for Nicole. David would have thought that if Nicole could see that Gina's success was largely dependent upon these systems, she might stick with them. And she did— for a whole week. But then she dropped back again.

He was starting to feel pretty ineffective with them. Oh sure, they were grateful for the creative features he came up with, the ideas he rolled off, the support he gave them in keeping the pressure on the administrative staff to keep up with the work, the computers he seemed to be able to squeeze from management. But his job was handling people, making them more successful.

David had to admit it to himself that he could manage the work, but he wasn't really managing the people. He knew he didn't inspire them, he wasn't changing the way they worked and often they simply avoided him. 'I wish someone could tell me what I'm doing wrong,' he muttered to himself.

Problems with other managers

It wasn't just his sales team that was causing him problems. It seemed to David that he spent as much time working around the other managers in the management team as he did with his own people. There were times when David seriously wondered if they were working for the same company.

Andre in the accounts department was always taking pot-shots at David's reps. He was always making comments about long, boozy client lunches and how they didn't know what hard work was. He judged them harshly and seemed to enjoy sending his people around to stir things up because a form hadn't been filled in correctly. There was very little give and take between the departments; it seemed to David that Andre's staff abruptly demanded and David's reps complied. This wasted a lot of time and every incident increased the resentment the reps felt.

The information technology department was always condescending, too. They were supposed to be teaching the reps how to use their new laptops, but it just wasn't happening. Sylvia, the manager of the department, didn't seem to understand what the salespeople needed. She was trying to make them work the way she wanted them to work, and it just wasn't practical. Sylvia wanted the reps to use the software she had picked and couldn't see that it was going to make them spend more time on administration. Sure, it would make life easier in the long run, but at what cost of daily and weekly time for the reps? It kept them off the road. But every time they tried to discuss it, they both became frustrated. David just couldn't get Sylvia to see his side of things.

And as for the creative department, they were supposed to be there to support sales. That was a joke. They were prima donnas who took offence if the client didn't like their creative concepts. It seemed to David that some of the creative people felt that the advertisers were wrong for wanting to sell products. But when he tried to address these issues with Sam, the creative director, he was always running out the door to go to a client meeting. David was never able to get any answers, from him. When he cornered him, the only answer David got was that he would talk to his people about it, but nothing ever changed. If David brought it up at a management meeting in an attempt to get the situation discussed, Sam would become very quiet. He'd sit there, head down, avoiding eye contact. This was very frustrating. David had talked about the situation with his general manager, and he had seemed just as frustrated with Sam. This wasn't too encouraging for David, because if the general manager couldn't do anything about him, what hope did David have?

Sometimes it seemed as if the managers were deliberately trying to make his job harder. He had to fight for things that obviously would make his department more effective, if not more efficient. And he included his boss in this. It seemed that some days, David quite simply got off-side with his boss. He couldn't explain it any other way. Some days, David just couldn't get through to him; either he wasn't communicating well or his boss just wasn't listening. David didn't know what it was that got in the way or what to do about it.

Problems at home

He was working long hours trying to make this work, but it didn't seem to help in the long run. It only made things worse at home. Shelley understood his need for recognition and was happy to allow for his ambition, but her patience was running short. She told him at the weekend that she felt he wasn't listening any more — not to her, and certainly not to the kids. David thought that was ironic. She was accusing him of doing what he was accusing his boss of doing. Maybe if he watched what his boss was doing to him, he could work out what he was doing wrong with his kids.

David thought about his kids for a moment. Justin was fifteen, Annie thirteen. His relationship with Justin was falling apart. Every time that David tried to communicate with his son, it seemed to get worse. Justin was either sullen or accused him of not listening or not understanding. And he was right, thought David. He didn't understand. He didn't understand his kids and why he couldn't have a reasonable conversation with them. He didn't understand why he couldn't identify what it was his reps were doing and how to improve it. He didn't understand why the management team didn't work together better instead of driving each other nuts all the time. And he didn't understand why he couldn't communicate better with his boss. He got on really well with all the clients, why couldn't he do that with others in the office?

'I wish someone could tell me what I'm doing wrong. I wish that someone would take all these people one by one and tell me how to handle them and how to make a difference.'

*

This book will tell you how to handle your people and how to make a difference. Read through the concepts and processes described here. You will find David's solutions for all these people problems in the epilogue.

1 THE 'NICE GUY'

From the moment we pick up our first favourite toy, we are trained to be 'nice'. We are taught to be fair. Heartbroken, we watch another child take possession of the toy dearest to our heart and we are supposed to be content, even happy that we have been able to share! In the midst of a raging fury and a sense of injustice, we learn that the greatest sin is to be selfish, to think of ourselves first. We're taught that we must be nice to others, to look after them, regardless of how we feel about it. Being nice helps keep everything calm and civilised. Being nice supports everyone and makes them happy. And that's what we're supposed to do — make others happy.

This behaviour solves some of the problems of human interaction, but it also creates some. We want to be nice, we want to be fair and give the other person the benefit of the doubt. We want to support them and show them we care. And if we are dealing with other Nice Guys, they will repay us by becoming more loyal and hardworking. They will come to like us more. True? Let's look at some examples and see if it really works that way.

Late for work

One of your staff is late for work and has been late every day this week. You reluctantly call her into your office and address the issue. She admits she's been late and, visibly upset, explains that she's having terrible arguments with her partner. You are sympathetic but firm, you understand she's having problems at home but she must try to get to work on time. You extract a promise from her and send her on her way.

You feel that you have addressed the situation calmly, fairly and firmly, with understanding and compassion, and that you have reminded her of her obligations to the company. The next day, much to your satisfaction, she is on time. The following day, she's running late again. You wonder what you did wrong. What did you miss?

Right intention, wrong application. Look back on your meeting with your staff member. Who did most of the talking? You did. Who dictated the promise for her to be on time? You did. What part did she take in the proceedings? She was upset because she had a problem at home, she listened to you and she agreed with you. But she also knows that you are a Nice Guy and she'd rather face your disapproval than confront the real problem. If changing is too much trouble for her, deep down she knows that you will let her off the hook. Again.

Because you are a Nice Guy, your problem with your staff member is likely to get worse. You may let her off the hook. If you do, you will have to address the situation further down the track when it has become an even bigger problem.

By letting her off the hook you will be sending her some powerful messages:

It's okay for her to let her personal life spill over into her work life.

Her arguments with her partner are more important than her professional image.

You think it's okay for her to be late as long as she has a good enough excuse.

Why would you let her off the hook? There are two reasons, and they are both because you are a Nice Guy. Firstly, you want to be supportive. Secondly, you don't want to upset anyone. You may feel that you are supporting her by not putting too much pressure on her while she is under stress at home. You think, she's upset, it would be better if I talk to her tomorrow when she's calmer. I'll talk to her when the time is right. And then tomorrow you are busy, so you decide to talk to her the next day. You are secretly hoping that by the time you get around to talking to her, the problem will have gone away.

By letting her off the hook, you are not supporting her in her work role; you are supporting her as an incapable person who can't get to work on time. You are saying, she isn't capable of looking after herself, I'll look after her. And that's how you may feel, that she needs looking after. But how has letting her off the hook actually helped her?

You see, your problem with your staff member is not that she is having problems with her partner, but that she isn't taking responsibility for getting to work on time. The arguments are almost irrelevant. They are a real problem for her, but, as far as getting to work on time is concerned, they are just the excuse. And if she doesn't take responsibility for getting to work on time now, she'll have other excuses when the arguments stop. The issue is how she behaves because of them.

There are two other issues here. Firstly, if your staff member is getting sympathy from the rest of the office with the drama in her life, she may not be interested in stopping the arguments, or changing the behaviour. Believe it or not, some people thrive on the attention they get when they are having problems. They mistake attention and sympathy for popularity. Playing the victim is very rewarding for them. If you have a potential victim on your hands, put strong standards in place and stop the clusters of sympathetic ears. She won't flourish under such a 'hostile' boss, and will either straighten up and get on with the job or she will leave.

Secondly, if she is sloppy about getting to work on time, she may well be sloppy in other areas. We carry our standards and ethics through all parts of our lives. We like to think that while we may do something not so well in one area of our lives, we do it better elsewhere in our lives. You might think that while you're late for work, you're seldom late in your private life. I'll bet your friends and family disagree! The positive side of this is that if we improve our ethics in one area, we generally tighten up in other areas. Small improvement in one area is usually followed by small improvements in other areas.

So how does letting her off the hook help her? It doesn't.

The emotional battery

Deep down, you already know this. So what stops you from dealing with the situation? Emotion. Yours. You imagine what is going to happen when you talk to her. You know that she is already upset and you imagine her bursting into tears in your office. You will feel embarrassed. She will think you are cold and unfeeling, and that's not your intention. You want to be understanding, but you need her to get to work on time. You don't want to upset her, but you know you need to say something. So you avoid it. Not deliberately, but you rationalise that you will find the right time, when you've got a moment. Or maybe you will call her in to the office, but will be more abrupt than you intended and hurry the interview to get her out of your office before she gets too upset and starts to cry.

It is your own emotion, and your imagination, that stops you from handling it properly. You feel uncomfortable at the thought of upsetting her further, and you want to avoid feeling uncomfortable. But by avoiding the emotion, you actually create a more emotionally fraught situation. What you avoid, you create.

What you avoid, you create.

If you avoid handling the issue, you will get angry and impatient every time she comes in late. The emotional pressure will build until you have to say something. And when you do you will be very angry. She will be mortified because she thought you didn't really mind, and now she finds that you did. And not only did you mind, but you've been watching and waiting and not saying anything. She will be really upset! You will have created exactly what you were trying to avoid.

Unexpressed emotion is like a battery. Don't say something and the battery starts to charge up. Something else comes up and the battery charges up a little more. She is late again. When you don't address it, the battery charges up still more. You come across a cluster of office staff comforting her in the corridor and walk by without saying anything. Frustration builds and the battery charges up even more. When she is late yet again it's like putting a spanner across the connections of the battery: kapow! Your reaction is extreme, and you say things that later you will regret.

Now, if you had said something in the first place, the battery wouldn't have charged up. Expressing what you feel in an appropriate way dissipates the energy and you feel calm afterwards. Don't say what you want to and you will continue to think about it, and continue to get annoyed well beyond what the situation deserves.

If you speak up now, in an appropriate way, you will be acknowledging that your staff member is capable of doing better. You will be able to work with her to achieve that result. You will be contributing to her becoming a more professional and valued employee. She will respect you for the result you will get, and you will certainly feel better about your handling of the situation.

So, you need to break through the hesitation created by your emotion and imagination. This takes practice, determination and a long-term point of view. It's very much like standing on the edge of a swimming pool. You've been gardening, and you're hot and dusty. You know the water is going to feel icy cold and you hesitate. Common sense and logic tell you that you'll feel better after a swim, but you still hesitate. Your imagination stops you. You imagine the shock of the cold water. You even shiver at the thought of it. Emotion and imagination are more powerful than thoughts or logic. It takes practice to learn that the result is worth it. If your intention is strong and you have a sense of long-term consequences, you dive in. The cold water makes you gasp, but you keep swimming. Soon you feel revitalised and refreshed, you feel great! You're pleased that you dived in.

> **Emotion and imagination are more powerful than thoughts or logic.**

It is your emotion that makes you hesitate. You have the best of intentions; you don't want to hurt or upset others. You need to take the long-term point of view. Will it be better or worse if you put off the discussion? Will it help your staff member if she faces the same situation again? Are you supporting her as a capable person? Or are you supporting her as an incapable person?

Handling the situation

So, how do you handle this kind of situation without being an ogre, firmly but with understanding, and encourage her to change?

Firstly, you have to get her to take responsibility for her behaviour. You have to get her to tell you what she's been doing that is not acceptable either to the firm or for her in the long run.

Secondly, she needs to tell you what should be happening, what she should be doing that she's not (arriving at work on time). Ask her what might stop her from getting to work on time. What things does she need to put into place to ensure she gets to work on time? When she thinks about this, she will run the likely events through her mind. She will imagine the emotions she might feel and the obstacles she might face, and she will prepare herself. We all know that role-plays allow us to prepare ourselves and handle things better, but we seldom do this with others who are struggling with a problem.

The things that you need to ask are:

- What should be happening?
- What do you need to do to make this happen?
- What's the first thing you need to do to make this happen?
- What might stop you?
- What do you need to do to ensure you continue the way you intend to?

In this case, your staff member needs to get to work on time. This means that she either has to stop arguing with her partner or ensure that she patches things up the night before. Or she may have to leave the argument behind her at home when she comes to work. That way she will catch the bus or train as she had planned.

The key is for her to take responsibility for what is happening to her. Then she will be able to commit to changing the behaviour that is unacceptable. Telling people that they have to change and getting them to agree to it is not going to change anything.

Change is only possible if she accepts the responsibility for the behaviour in the first place.

> **Telling people that they have to change and getting them to agree to it is not going to change anything.**

Once she has accepted the responsibility, she needs a strong reason to change. Walk her down the long-term consequences of her behaviour. As her boss, you will get impatient and dissatisfied with her. She may even lose her job. How will that help her cope with her problems? It must only make things worse.

You can support her and be understanding, but not at the expense of dropping the standards. You can be most supportive by maintaining standards and helping her become more professional.

Struggling to make budget

Picture this. One of your salespeople is struggling to make budget and you have been watching him for a while, trying to figure out what he's doing wrong. Finally, you spot it and call him into your office to have a chat. You ask him what he thinks is not working for him and patiently listen to his excuses, but you already know what he's doing wrong. He's not closing strongly at the end of the sale.

Now, you got the job as sales manager because you were good at sales and you know exactly what your salesperson needs to do. So you tell him. You tell him what he's not doing and, encouraged by him nodding his head in embarrassed agreement, you tell him what you would do if you were in his shoes. You go over some specific examples to demonstrate to him how successful your techniques were, you check that he understands and send him on his way. You feel pleased with yourself because you have just done your job exceptionally well. You have identified the problem, given him the solution, motivated and encouraged him and sent him back out there to try it for himself. Right? Wrong.

Chances are that your salesperson will go out there with good intentions and give it a try. Chances are that nothing will change and he will continue to try to make sales without closing. Or he may decide that your method works for you, but he and his customers are different and what you have told him doesn't apply to them. But he won't tell you this. He'll just continue on his own way of doing things and, again, nothing will change. I'm not saying that if he could see a way of changing that was acceptable to him, he wouldn't try it, but you haven't given him one.

Think about it. Your solution to the problem is not necessarily the right solution for the person who has the problem. And that's the whole point! It's not you who has the problem. Your salesperson thinks differently, acts differently and feels differently about what he does.

> **Your solution to the problem is not necessarily the right solution for the person who has the problem.**

Who did most of the talking? You. Who dictated the solution? You. What part did your salesperson take in the proceedings? He was embarrassed because he knew he was doing something wrong. He listened to you, and he agreed with you. But do you know why he isn't closing strongly at the end of the sale? Perhaps he thinks that the product is too expensive and feels uncomfortable charging that much. Perhaps he feels he is putting pressure on people. If he's a Nice Guy, closing the sale may feel as if he is pushing and he won't want to threaten the relationship. You don't know why he isn't closing strongly at the end of the sale. And if you don't know, how can you help him?

Can you see that, with the best intention in the world, you are being the Nice Guy again and solving his problem for him? How have you made him take responsibility? Have you got a commitment from him or just an agreement with what you are saying?

You need to find out what your salesperson thinks should be happening. What stops him? It is what stops him that you have to address. If you can't get him to identify what stops him, you need to read immediately the chapter in this book on listening skills. Cancel all your appointments, close your office door and read that chapter on listening skills — you are not getting to the real problem. You are simply addressing the problem you would have if you were in his shoes.

Handling the real problem will make you the best sales manager the company has ever had, because so few managers are able to do this. Remember, emotion and imagination are more powerful than thoughts or logic. So, even though you have given your salesperson a logical explanation of how to solve his problem, he still feels bad about doing it. He will not follow your advice. He will continue to do it his way, even though it is proving not to be a successful way of operating. You have to find out how he feels and what it is he is avoiding.

Getting past the excuses
Whenever we do something we shouldn't or do something we feel uncomfortable about, we have to make it okay with ourselves. So we rationalise what we do. We justify why we had to do it that way. And when explaining this to another person we are convincing. We're convincing because we have talked ourselves into believing our rationalisations. We have to in order to feel okay about what we've done.

Actually, deep down we don't feel okay, but we don't want to look too closely, because either we don't have the solution, or the solution wasn't palatable to us at the time and we took the easy way out. For whatever reason, when we are questioned as to why we did things that way, we trot out the rationalisations, the justifications, the excuses. And the Nice Guy accepts them as real. But, as we're starting to see, believe these excuses and you're not getting to the real problem.

So, how do you spot when someone's giving you excuses? Often they will give you two, three, four, even five excuses, one after the other. It only takes one thing to stop us. If you get two or three excuses one after the other, know that's just what they are, excuses, and keep asking questions.

> **If you get two or three excuses one after the other, know that's just what they are, excuses, and keep asking questions.**

I was working with a sales manager who was having difficulty with one of her staff who consistently demonstrated behaviour that she felt was unacceptable. Up until that point, she had not addressed it. At the start of our session, she burst out with a description of how the staff member had done it again and how frustrated she was with him. I asked her if she had addressed it with him. She said she hadn't and explained why, and absolutely assured me that the next time she saw him do this again she'd handle it. She'd talk to him and make him aware, in no uncertain terms, that this was unacceptable to her. She was very convincing, but I was more interested in what had stopped her, not what she was going to do in the future. If you don't do something different, whatever stops you this time will also stop you next time.

> **If you don't do something different, whatever stops you this time will also stop you next time.**

'So, why didn't you talk to him?' I asked her.

'There was nowhere private where I could talk to him,' she said. 'I was really busy, so was he, and it was his birthday.'

So, she had four reasons for not addressing this situation with him.

I decided to address each excuse, one at a time. 'You had nowhere private to talk to him? What about the room we're in now? What was wrong with this room?'

'Someone was using it.' At this point, she still believes her rationalisations.

'And you couldn't find an office anywhere else in the whole building that you could use?'

'Well, I suppose if I had gone looking I could have found one. But I was really busy at that time and he was flat out, too.'

'But didn't you tell me that the next time he behaved like that you would have an example to use to address his behaviour? And so you needed to do it immediately?'

'Yes, I did. But it was his birthday.'

17

She's starting to realise that there's something wrong with her justifications, and she's starting to feel uncomfortable.

'So, explain to me how the fact that it's his birthday makes a difference.'

'Well, I don't know about you,' sarcasm slips in as she starts to get defensive — we must be getting close, this is a last attempt to put me off, 'but I think birthdays should be happy days, not days where someone upsets you.'

'So, you think that addressing his behaviour and making him a more valuable employee is going to upset him?'

'Not when you put it that way, no.'

'But you felt he was going to get upset if you addressed this behaviour with him?'

'Yes, of course I did.'

'So what were you really trying to avoid?'

She gave me a shocked look, thought for a moment, grinned and said, 'I was trying to avoid upsetting him. And of course, when I finally do talk to him, I'll be so frustrated, I will upset him more.'

Now she knows what she's really dealing with. She's avoiding conflict and doesn't want to upset her staff. She's a typical Nice Guy, but now her awareness has lifted on why she behaves the way she does and what she's trying to avoid. If she keeps a long-term perspective on her staff, focuses on helping them grow and improve, and understands that it's her fear of conflict that kicks in and stops her, she's got a far better chance of pushing through to get a good result.

Another way of identifying if the person is handing you excuses, is to ask yourself, does this make sense? She said that she had no place in which to talk to him. Are you expected to believe that in the whole building there was not one room where she could have had a private talk with him? And if this was the case, surely they could have gone to a local coffee shop and discussed this over coffee. But, of course, this solution wouldn't have been acceptable to her if she thought he was going to get upset. Now it makes sense; once you have the real problem, it makes complete sense. But until then, it doesn't.

> **Another way of identifying if the person is handing you excuses, is to ask yourself, does this make sense?**

She was busy? What's she supposed to do, wait until she's got nothing to do before she can address issues with her staff? She's paid to be busy! She's meant to be busy for most of her day. Even when she's planning and thinking, essential parts of her job, she's still busy. Starting to get the picture? If it doesn't make sense, ask the person to explain it to you. In the effort to explain the thinking process to you, you will see the lack of logic or the weakness; you may even spot what it is that the person is trying to avoid. If a situation is not being addressed, chances are that the person is trying to avoid something unpleasant. In other words, that person might be a Nice Guy like you.

The Nice Guy pendulum
Now, you may be saying to yourself, well, some of this fits, but I'm not a Nice Guy because I am tough on some people. And that's the double whammy of Nice Guys, they're toughest on themselves and those closest to them. They'll demand high standards, have high expectations, and will be tough on people close to them and with themselves.

But when it comes to negative people or people with problems, Nice Guys will swing the other way. They will want to help. They can't stand the thought of anyone being upset or hurt. They'll know what people in trouble need to do to get out of trouble. They'll start to give them solutions, and bingo, they're hooked! They've latched themselves on to a problem person and they'll bend over backwards to be 'fair', but all the while they are being manipulated by the problem person. Their good intentions will ensure that they are softest on those who cause them the most problems. Eventually, they will be forced to handle them and, chances are, they will then go over the top. They'll be left wondering what they did wrong. What they did wrong was to try to help a person who wanted the problem more than the solution. Nice Guys look at the wrong thing. They look at the problem. They should be looking at what the person is doing to create the situation.

Nice Guys look at the wrong thing. They look at the problem. They should be looking at what the person is doing to create the situation.

To identify if you've fallen into this trap, look around you and see if you have people you help who are unable to help you in return. In other words, if you've been helping a sales rep and, after a reasonable period of time, the rep still isn't helping you by achieving budget, take another look at the situation. Put aside the excuses both you and the rep believe in, and look at what is stopping the rep from achieving. What is it the rep is doing that is contributing to the situation? Nice Guys usually only see one point of view, that of the person in trouble. But there's another side to the story. Take a good hard look.

Summary
Encourage other people to take responsibility for their behaviour. Get them to tell you:
- what they've been doing that is not acceptable either to the firm or to themselves in the long run
- what should be happening
- what they need to do to make this happen
- what the first step is that they need to take to make sure that this happens
- what might stop them

- what they need to do to ensure they continue through with their intention.

Ask yourself whether you have:
- helped make them more capable
- got to the heart of the problem or simply addressed the excuses.
- Worked harder for them for them than they have themselves.

2 PROBLEM PEOPLE

Is there someone in your team who claims a lot of your attention? Does someone seem to be on your mind most of the time? Does someone have a problem that you help solve and it is quickly followed by another problem? Your good people get the job done and achieve good results. This person may also get good results, but there are always dramas.

Assess how much time you spend with each person in your department. Get an accurate picture of how much time you spend with each of them or worrying about each of them. If you find there are one or two who claim too much of your time and attention, the chances are you have a problem person on your hands. And, let's face it, you've got enough to do without constantly having to attend to one or two people above all the others in your department.

Problem people may be in the wrong job, or this behaviour may be an indication of how they live their lives. Problem people take your attention off the things you do successfully to put time and effort into handling them. They may use a camouflage of niceness, but these people have a hidden agenda that is destructive to your plans, your relationships or your team.

> **Problem people take your attention off the game and move it onto their problem.**

The reason managers spend so much time on problem people is that they can appear to be indispensable. The first rule of business is to get rid of anyone who is indispensable. If you consider one of your staff to be indispensable, this means that their presence in your business is essential, that it can't operate without them. This makes your business reliant on that person and dangerously vulnerable. What happens if they go on holiday, get hit by a bus, or, even worse, go to work for your competitors?

In a business situation, there are two kinds of problem people. One achieves target but takes a huge chunk of time and attention. Looking over the team results at the end of the month, you'll probably reassure yourself that maybe all the time and attention was worth it. That's why these people are so hard to handle — at the end of the day, they produce. If they weren't producing good results, you would have had a reason to get rid of them by now. But you haven't, because the bottom line is that they achieve budget. But at what cost for you and the other staff in your department? Is it really worth it? Imagine if you had someone producing the same results without taking so much of your time and attention during the month.

The other type of problem people don't perform, but you know they are capable of it. You may be particularly fond of these people and want to see them do well. They show glimpses of their capabilities and you want to support them. You know they can do it and they say all the right things. You hope this is the month they are going to make it. But deep down, you have a sneaking suspicion that they won't, as much as you'd like them to. Or if they do, you suspect that the following month they'll miss budget again.

It's important to understand how problem people operate. They attack what *you* do so that you don't focus on what they're doing. You present the new budget to your sales team. Your good people may comment that the budgets are high, but they'll give it their best shot. The problem person will accuse you of being interested only in the dollars. In all sorts of subtle ways, problem people make you feel sorry for them. Fancy having to work for a boss who's only interested in the dollars! And because there's an element of truth in what they say (of course you're interested in achieving budget), you back off. That's not how you want to be, or how you want your staff to perceive you. You realise that somehow you've been side tracked, but you now feel uncomfortable about handling them.

Problem people are very good at generalising. 'Everybody thinks you're too tough!' You imagine a wave of condemnation about you. In fact, it is only the problem person and that person's friends, and usually only one sympathiser at that. But problem people manage to make it sound as if the whole office is talking about you behind your back and has banded together in agreement about your faulty management of them.

Problem people always talk about what they've done in the past and what they're going to do in the future. They'll remind you of the great record they had at their last job and walk you through all the things they have in the pipeline.

Problem people create confusion around the results they are getting and live on hope. They get caught in their own PR and exaggeration, and resist at all costs focusing on the results they are getting now. If their results are down and you discuss this with them, they'll side track you by pointing out your violations to take your focus off their present behaviour.

Problem people may also compulsively avoid confronting reality, which makes it difficult, if not impossible, for a manager to handle them. I was working with a woman I considered to be a problem person and asked her if she had achieved budget for the month. Firmly and convincingly, she assured me that she had. Now, I knew that she had missed budget and was intrigued that she could claim she had achieved it.

'Really? You got budget this month? Are you sure?'

'Yes, of course I'm sure,' she said, smiling and looking a little sideways at me. Now, this would stop most people asking any further. By the slight movement of her head, she is indicating that I am asking silly questions.

But I knew she hadn't got budget! 'But I was under the impression that you had missed budget this month.'

'No, I got budget this month.'

After a slight hesitation, she then said, 'Of course, I lost Skyzone's order. But before they cancelled, I did have budget.' And she launched into the story of how another rep had stolen Skyzone from her. It was someone else's fault, she was just the poor victim. Later, her manager was amazed at the accuracy of my prediction that within the next week she would be away with a migraine. In fact, I predicted that when she did get budget, she wouldn't cope with the success anyway and would again fall victim to a migraine. I was right both times. If you are locked into this pattern, you won't allow yourself to have success. So when things do go well, problem people will go to extraordinary lengths to get themselves back into trouble so that you can feel sorry for them again. And so that they can feel sorry for themselves.

Problem people will try to distract you from focusing on their results by telling you about the things you do wrong or about what the other reps or managers are doing to them. Once you have identified what they are doing, ignore the feelings of sympathy which will flood to the surface, and remain focused on the issue of their results.

Problem people will try to distract you from focusing on their results by telling you about the things you do wrong or about what the other reps or managers are doing to them.

Another technique problem people use is to get you to take on their problems as your own. You can't solve them because they aren't your problems. You can run around trying to solve the problems, but you will be wasting your time. You will feel inadequate, which means that when they so kindly point out your shortfalls — 'Everyone thinks you're too tough!' — you'll feel that they could be right. If you're a Nice Guy, this will distract you and you'll seriously examine the truth of it. Your attention is now on whether you are too tough and off the results the problem people are achieving, or not achieving. They will have distracted you from addressing their behaviour by getting you to focus on an element of truth about yours. This creates emotional confusion for you, and your judgement will become even more flawed around them. But your behaviour and how they feel about it isn't the issue here.

Problem people reduce your certainty and create foggy thinking. You knew exactly what to do, but since talking to them, you're not so sure anymore.

Problem people reduce your certainty and create foggy thinking.

For example, Alan comes to you with the complaint, 'Kate really annoys me when she makes personal phone calls.' You don't have a problem with the calls Kate makes because she keeps them short. But you ask her to keep her calls to a minimum. Then Alan finds something else about Kate that bothers him. You chase up this new problem to attempt to fix it. After all, you are trying to create a happy, motivated team. But what about Alan? What is he trying to create? Is he taking responsibility for the relationship by running to you to fix it for him? The fact is, it isn't your problem. You should simply say, 'Well, what are you going to do about it? You'd better handle that with Kate.'

Problem people take your attention off the game and move it onto their problem. They don't take responsibility, they blame — usually you, if you're the one bringing a problem to their attention.

Problem people take your attention off the things you do successfully to put time and effort into handling them.

Problem people and illness

Be alert for problem people putting the blame on illness. If they haven't achieved their budget it may be because they were away with a migraine, a cold or some other illness. Monitor their sick days and identify whether they get ill with surprising regularity. Then go back and insist on them achieving budget. If your best people were close to achieving budget and they didn't feel well, they would drag themselves to work and make it happen despite the illness.

Problem people won't. Anything will stop them and they'll condemn you for insisting on them achieving budget and not having sympathy for their situation. But why do problem people get ill so regularly? Problem people are often people in the wrong job. Most of us have at some time or another been in a job we didn't like, or worked for a boss we disliked. Can you remember what that was like? It's depressing. You feel unhappy, resentful and critical. You focus on all the things you don't like about the place, and what you focus on magnifies. You complain to anyone who will listen, and disassociate yourself from all the potentially good things about your situation.

Studies show that stress and unhappiness weaken our immune system and we are more prone to illness. Because we feel low, we have less energy. Everything takes more effort. We drag ourselves around, feeling sorry for ourselves, and before we know it, that attitude becomes the norm for us. It's not until we step out of an unhappy situation that we realise how much it was affecting us. If you put a frog in a pot of boiling water, it will be out of that pot with one super-motivated bound. But if you put it in a pot of warm water that it feels comfortable in and slowly turn up the heat, it will get used to the hotter water. Turn it up again and it will adjust again. You will be able to boil the water and the frog won't have jumped out.

That's the way it is with unhappiness. We become unhappy, and this level becomes normal for us. Slowly, it gets worse and we get used to that, until we are desperately unhappy. But it feels completely normal, so we don't do anything about changing our circumstances. Once out of the situation, we can be horrified how desperately unhappy we were without realising it.

I've seen people get sick time after time until their illness forced them to give up the job they hated. You work it out.

On the other side of the coin, when we're in a job we love, we're motivated, we have huge amounts of creativity and energy, and nothing can stop us achieving what we are aiming for. And we seldom get sick.

Problem people as victims

Problem people get you to focus on their loss rather than their results. Which of these people would you rather have working for you: those who see obstacles as a challenge to be overcome, or the 'poor me, it wasn't my fault' problem people? Remember, if it wasn't their fault, there's nothing they can do about it! And so they remain helpless, seeking your sympathy. And if you're a Nice Guy, you'll want to jump in and rescue them.

If you jump in and rescue them, you may temporarily fix the problem, but, in reality, nothing will have changed. Whatever they did to get themselves into that situation is still in place, and, if they continue with the same behaviour, they'll end up in the same situation. They'll have the same problem to deal with all over again.

By rescuing them, you are saying, 'You're not capable of solving this problem yourself, I'll support you as an incapable being and fix it for you.' Having shown them how much you love and support them, you might even admit to yourself that it would be nice for them to show some gratitude. But have you noticed that it never seems to work quite that way?

Problem people don't appreciate your help. They may even blame you when the next problem comes along. Have you ever heard 'It's all your fault' when you were only trying to help? You end up feeling like a victim of your own good deeds, feeling like the bad guy. After all you did for them, this is how they thank you.

When you look back on it, you'll see how you found some way to get your own back. Whether it was sarcasm, 'I told you so', proving them wrong, sacking them or withholding yourself from them for a while.

The game in its most basic form goes like this. If you feel something is being done to you (victim), you will want to punish (persecute) the doer. You'll want to make them feel as bad as you do. Then you can rescue them (rescuer) and make it all okay again. Until the next time. Rescuer-victim-persecutor: the bad news is that if you play one role you will play all three.

> **Rescuer–victim–persecutor: the bad news is that if you play one role you will play all three.**

The *Collins English Dictionary* defines 'rescue' as 'to save'. By its very meaning it implies that the other person is helpless. And you may feel they are. But how does what you've done help them if they have to face this problem again? How do you help an alcoholic, an addict or a co-dependent person? Not by preventing   the next drink or the next fix, not by nagging them and telling them what they already know, but by getting them to admit they have a problem. If they won't admit they have a problem, then the problem is all yours. What are you going to do about it?

How do you identify if you're in the role of rescuer? Look for a strong sense of doing the right thing for someone. Maybe you believe you know best what is good for them, or you know exactly what they should do. You may even believe that you make better decisions than they do.

The *Collins English Dictionary* defines 'victim' as 'a person who suffers harm from another, a person who is tricked or swindled'. To victimise is to punish or to discriminate against someone unfairly. And feeling that something's unfair is the key indicator that tells you you're in this game.

The dictionary definition of 'persecutor' is 'to oppress, harass or maltreat'. Nagging is a form of persecution. We nag people to do what we know is the best thing for them to do.

Problem people appear to be nice people
Problem people can use a camouflage of niceness. Sometimes they are hard to spot because you can't believe that such a 'nice' person could be so manipulative. They can also appear to be so positive that you will miss that they are actually negative. Think about it, how does Alan coming to you and complaining about Kate support the team? It doesn't, it undermines the team spirit. So while he might dress it in a syrup of 'trying to make a better team', he is creating conflict and not taking responsibility for solving that conflict.

Problem people and scarcity
Problem people 'run scarcity'. In other words, if someone in the team is a high achiever, that means that there is less for the problem person in the marketplace. Problem people are locked into the win–lose situation. If there's a winner, there must be a loser, and it's usually them. Stop and think about this for a moment. This means they believe that the whole team can't achieve budget together, and certainly can't all over-achieve. Do you really want to have on your team a player who doesn't believe that the whole team can win? This attitude will undermine the others in all sorts of subtle ways. Imagine the effect on the rest of the team and how much harder you will have to work on their motivation.

How to handle problem people
Why are problem people so difficult to handle? Some of the problems will be created by the problem people, but some will be caused by you making errors of judgement because of the emotional confusion they create.

The first step is to identify how they hook you into playing their game. Nice Guys are the easiest prey for problem people; Nice Guys bend over backwards to be 'fair'. Nice Guys will listen to what problem people say and seriously examine their complaints and comments. Usually, Nice Guys then think about their own behaviour or management style. This results in them taking responsibility for something that is not their problem.

You say to one of your salespeople, 'You haven't met budget this month.'

She says, 'You've set the budgets unfairly. I've got a really small client base.'

You immediately begin to wonder if, in fact, what you asked of her was unreasonable. You are falling into the trap. You need to keep your focus on the result you are looking for and not allow yourself to be side tracked into wondering whether the budget was unreasonable. The trick is to insist on your salesperson achieving budget. It will either straighten her up or get rid of her.

When problem people throw an accusation at you, like this salesperson did, take what you had said to her and imagine saying it to the best salesperson you have. What would her reaction be? You will immediately see that it is not you, but the reaction of the problem person that is at fault.

You say, 'You haven't met budget this month.'

She says, 'I didn't get budget because I have such a small client base. I need to get cracking and do some cold calling to build up my base. Do you have any ideas about how I could build it?'

She will take responsibility for doing something about it. She might ask for your help, but she won't attempt to blame you.

Another technique in dealing with problem people is to do something totally unexpected and apparently irrational. You see, problem people think they know you well enough to predict how you will react in a given situation. If you are normally nice and reasonable, become unreasonable in your demands. If you normally do all the talking, tell them what you want, ask them how they are going to achieve it, and then clam up.

To avoid being caught in the rescuer–victim–persecutor game, refuse to rescue problem people. Firstly, confront the emotion you feel about their problem. What feeling would have kicked in if you'd said, 'No, I won't do this for you'? Secondly, why would it be a problem for you to say: 'But I will help you do it yourself'? They don't think the problem is as bad as you say? They can't be bothered? They think they can't do it themselves?

To solve the problem for them is to support them as incapable beings. The ethical thing to do is to support them as capable beings and encourage them to take responsibility for the consequences of their actions. Once they have done that, only then can you guide them through the steps they need to take to solve their problem.

You need to spot how you feel around problem people. Often when you feel down it's because you have just been dealing with one. Remember how negative they really are. If you try to help problem people, you will fail and will end up feeling useless. Understand that this is what keeps problem people's games going.

If problem people are undermining you and your team, look on them as the enemy until they prove otherwise. Don't support them by being nice to them.

We are all capable of behaving like problem people if we're in a situation we don't like or a job we don't feel suited to. Instead of being responsible and doing something about it, we demonstrate that we aren't happy and create situations where we draw attention to ourselves. Moving on can sometimes be the best possible outcome for all involved. A person may demonstrate problem person behaviour in one job and be a shining example of the model employee in another situation with a different product or management. It is the behaviour, the attitude and the lack of responsibility that creates the problem. Your reaction to problem people and your management of them confirms the problem.

Problem people as managers

Up until now, I have been talking about problem people within your staff. But it is just as likely that you could have problem people in your management team. Managers who will always say it can't be done, and go out of their way to prove it to you are problem people. Managers who agree with your staff when they complain about your decisions are problem people — 'But what can I do? My hands are tied.' Make no mistake, they will have any number of subtle ways in which to undermine your authority and the team spirit. And there's nothing so demoralising to a team as to have disharmony or discord within the management team. Teams need to feel that regardless of what they think about the decisions that are made, management know how to make good long-term decisions. If one manager appears to have doubts, this can destroy the team sense of security and, ultimately, create a negative and critical environment.

And how do you handle managers who are problem people? In the same way you handle any other problem person: keep your focus on the issue and don't let yourself be side-tracked.

Problem people as clients

For some reason, it is always much easier spotting problem people who are clients. They don't value what you do for them, even though you may have spent far more time and energy handling them and their demands than you would for most of your other clients. And you also waste a lot of time handling their complaints or haggling over the bill at the end of the day.

There's only one question to ask yourself — are they worth it? Do they bring in enough revenue to the company to warrant you spending so much time and grief handling them? I very much doubt it. Most of the client problem people I have come across are either very small with an inflated idea of their value to you, or they are problem people within a client company. I know of several examples where, once the client problem person has been identified and the rep has discussed the situation with the manager, the manager has told the rep to stop giving in to their demands and treat them like any other client. Amazingly, this is often all it takes with some clients to get them to toe the line and back off from their unreasonable complaints and demands.

If the client company is a large one you can't afford to lose, your manager could pay a visit to the problem person's manager. Whether your manager actually addresses the problems you are having with the problem person, or simply builds a relationship with the client manager that you can casually drop into the conversations with the problem person, is a judgement for you to make.

Don't be intimidated by confronting the manager of a client problem person. I have done this in the past and it worked well. All circumstances are different, however, and you must decide what the most effective method is. Simply not complying with the problem person's demands may mean that you lose that client to your competitors. With any luck, you can kill two birds with one stone.

Problem people as friends

Friends as problem people are often the hardest to spot because you assume that, as friends, they are being supportive of you. Any criticism they give you is for your own good. But take a close look at what happens when you tell them about a new idea you have which will help you become more successful. Let's say that you decide to take a night class in a subject you feel you need to know more about. You tell your friend all about it enthusiastically as you visualise the results of doing the course. Your friend asks you how much the course is going to cost and how much of your valuable time it's going to take. Then, with a puzzled look, your friend asks, 'Why would you want to do this?' You find yourself explaining further, your enthusiasm waning a little.

Now, your friend hasn't said anything negative yet, only questioned you and got you to explain fully why you are considering doing this course. But, as you begin to explain, your friend doesn't return your enthusiasm. You begin to doubt the wisdom of your decision. You become less sure you're doing the right thing. You are suddenly uncertain about the whole idea. You have just been worked on by a master problem person! Note that your friend hasn't criticised you in any way; you are now doubting yourself.

A client told me about a friend who had been in his life for more than ten years. He said they supported each other through frustrations about lack of money, through uncertainty about their individual careers and through family upheavals. Their mutual support was unconditional and, therefore, all the more valuable. Then he bought his own business. He worked long hours, six days a week, and was motivated by every minute. He admitted that his life was a little out of balance and he consciously worked on exercising and taking time off, but on the whole he was very happy with the way things were going. He had money in the bank, clients he admired and loved working with, and a fantastic relationship with his wife and two sons. What more could he ask for?

Until his friend phoned him, 'How are things going?'

With great delight, my client told him about some of the new successes in his business and how good he felt about everything.

'You know, I'm worried about you. These days, every time I ask you how you are, you tell me how the business is going. It concerns me that you're becoming obsessed with it. It's taking over your life.'

Now, there was more than a grain of truth to what he was saying and that's how his friend the problem person hooked him in. There was some truth in what he said, so my client looked inwards and started searching for what he was doing wrong. In this case, the only thing he could think of that he was doing wrong was that he was being successful and having to consciously create more time for himself in his life. So he looked at the source of the advice, his friend. Broke, no idea where he was going in life and trying to come to terms with the breakup of a 15-year-long relationship. Now, none of these things diminishes him as a friend, but if his advice was valuable to my client, he would be a living example of what my client wanted to find in his life.

Our friends are chosen because of how comfortable we feel around them. When something changes, such as one person becoming more successful, often the discomfort experienced by the other can lead to the other person behaving like a problem person. When you address it, one of two things will happen. Your friend will become more aware about what she or he is doing and remain your friend or will disappear from your life and leave you to continue on your increasingly successful way.

The best solution is not to connect up with problem people as friends, staff, managers or clients in the first place.

Summary

To spot problem people:

- Take a step back and identify whether it is easy or difficult to get the results you are looking for from these people.
- Are you happy to invest the time, attention and energy in handling problem people and their problems?

- Do these people sometimes leave you feeling unsure of yourself?
- How supportive is their behaviour, of you, of the team?

To handle problem people:

- Keep your focus on the issue at hand and don't get side-tracked. If other issues arise, make a note of them and deal with them later, but keep focused at all costs.
- Avoid rescuing problem people by solving their problems for them.
- Insist on the result you want them to achieve and stay firm, disregarding for the moment any comments they make against you.
- Don't be nice or bend over backwards to be 'fair' to them. This is ammunition to problem people. Treat them as you would treat your good people or clients and expect the same results.

3 THE LAWS OF REAL VALUE

Tom Peters, one of the top authorities on business management, says, 'Your staff are energetic, caring, thorough and dedicated — except for the eight hours a day they work for you.' How do you get motivated, responsible staff? How do you get people who have initiative, who are motivated to go that extra mile for the customer? We all know that customers judge businesses by the staff they encounter. If your receptionist is busy and is a little curt, your customers will decide that your business doesn't care about its customers. If your salespeople are busy and forget to send the information they said they would send the next day, your customers will decide that your product or service is unreliable, not just your staff. Your customers will regard how your staff treat them as a reflection of your business.

You can talk and train until you're blue in the face but, ultimately, the motivation to give a superior service can't come from you, your people must be motivated to do it themselves. Giving a superior service must be as important to them as it is to you. So, how do you do this?

Have you seen companies who have loyal, highly motivated people working for them? Funnily enough, they also seem to be having a good time. What do these companies do to achieve this? Is it just luck?

If you look closely, you'll see that it often leads back to one individual within the company, usually the person at the top. These people have a knack of caring for and motivating others. They create intense loyalty. Their people will be so highly focused on the success of the company that they'll tolerate a high level of under-resourcing or frustration and will take exceptionally heavy workloads with very little complaint. They will do this as long as they feel valued by the person who is creating this loyalty.

This is what we are looking for when we talk about synergy and real teamwork. These people have unconsciously discovered the secret to the laws of real value. Their staff feel valued. When you feel valued, you will do whatever it takes to get a particular result. You are motivated, energetic and usually happy because you are contributing to a cause or a bigger picture. You are alive and feel valuable because you are making a contribution to some- thing that is bigger than you. A company or department that is creating outstanding results has created an environment where every person, from the support or administration team, through sales and into management, believes. Whether they believe in the product, the service, an idea, or just a dream, they all share it, with a passion. When people believe in a company, that belief sustains them through obstacles, rejection and lean times. They continue to reaffirm the belief when one of them gets low — they get them going again. And they convert everyone else they meet. Their belief in themselves and their product or service snowballs, both internally and externally.

This is what all the vision statements, the mission statements and the goal-setting workshops are trying to achieve. The mistake they make is that while you can create motivation and leave people feeling warm and fuzzy, it takes a champion of the cause within the company to ensure that this swell of motivation and belief continues and grows on a daily basis.

There is good news: this result comes from a concept so simple that, once you are aware of it, you can apply it to your staff and your customers. In fact, you can apply it to your relationships with your partner and your children. This concept builds strong and loyal relationships. Let's take it back to its simplest form before we look at how it works in the business arena.

A little boy's bike

Let's say that you decided when you were young that you wanted a bike. All the kids in the neighbourhood have a bike and, your nose pressed against the window of the local bike shop, you spot a dream of purple and red with wide tyres that would jet propel you to the height of your ambition. You race home and describe to your Dad how badly you need this bike, and you are so eloquent that you convince yourself, if not him, that even your school results would soar if you could just own this bike. Dad, trying to be a responsible parent, doesn't mind you owning the bike, but, knowing that nothing of value in life comes easy, he cuts you a deal. 'You earn half the money, and I'll pay for the rest.'

You haggle, but he remains firm. So you start looking for ways to earn some money. Now, one thing becomes very clear: Dad is the only person around the place who has any money to speak of. So you start watching him so you can work out what you can do that he'll pay well for. You are looking from the point of view of what's in it for him. You are on the positive cycle of the laws of real value.

> **You are looking from the point of view of what's in it for him. You are on the positive cycle of the laws of real value.**

It's breakfast time Friday morning. Dad's trying to read the paper before he heads off for the day. Mum puts his breakfast in front of him and casually mentions, 'Aunt Katya's coming to visit on Sunday.'

Dad puts down the paper, pricks his egg and watches, satisfied, as it flows across the toast before he answers. 'Dear old Aunt Katya, how is she? Still as picky as ever?'

'Andrew!' Your mother's warning is only half-hearted. 'But it does raise the point of the lawns. You were going to mow the lawns last weekend. I know you've got the kids' sport on tomorrow morning, so you'll have to mow them tomorrow afternoon.'

Seeing your opportunity, you announce, 'But Mum, Dad's going to watch the Eagles tomorrow afternoon! He can't mow the lawns then!'

Dad's echoed agreement encourages you on. 'Tell you what though, Dad. How about if I mow the lawns for you? For ten bucks.'

Dad's fork stops mid-air, he looks at you, considering. He goes through a two-step process. Does he have a want or a need? Yes, the lawns have to be mowed by the time Aunt Katya arrives Sunday afternoon. But his next consideration is the key one. Would he value paying ten dollars for you to mow it for him?

He decides that you're showing initiative, obviously taking after his side of the family. He nods his head, 'You've got a deal, son.'

Excited, you attack the lawn with vigour and do your ten- year-old best. Come inspection time, Dad can see that the edges haven't been done. In fact, it's not quite the way that Dad would have done the job, but he hands over the ten dollars, smiles and says, 'You've done a good job, son. I'm proud of you.' High praise from a normally reserved Dad. You're feeling pretty good now and you race inside to show your Mum your ten-dollar note to find that she's pretty happy with you, too. In fact, she slips you some of the cake she's baked for Aunt Katya and swears you to secrecy.

Whenever we demonstrate our competence, we feel good about ourselves and the world in general. Our self-esteem goes up, we become more energetic, more motivated to improve further and become more creative. This leads to the ability to make this happen again.

If it worked so well with Dad, maybe it would work for the neighbours, too! You go next door and pour out the whole story and not only do you get the lawns to mow, you get to clean out their garage as well. In a short time, you have a lawn-mowing business in your street, you've got a paper run and you're on constant demand for odd jobs. Ultimately, you get your bike. But there's one more part of this concept to be aware of. Some of your friends, eyeing your magnificent purple machine, tell you how lucky you are. They don't have a cool Dad like you do. You try to explain how it works, but they don't seem to listen. They just know that if only things were different, they'd be as 'lucky' as you. But you know that if only they were to apply the laws of real value, and work as hard as you have, they'd be as lucky as you. As the old saying goes, 'The harder I work, the luckier I get.'

When it all goes wrong
There are some fundamental parts of this concept, which, if left out or changed, turn the whole scenario around to a most unsatisfactory conclusion for all concerned.

Remember the beginning of the scenario? Your Mum was saying, 'You were going to mow those lawns last weekend. I know you've got the kid's sport on tomorrow morning, so you'll have to mow them tomorrow afternoon.'

But this time, you don't ask, you just make up your mind that mowing those lawns is a way in which you can get some money. Your attitude is coming from what's in it for me. You are on the negative cycle of the laws of real value.

> **Your attitude is coming from what's in it for me. You are on the negative cycle of the laws of real value.**

So, without asking Dad, you attack the lawn with vigour and do your ten-year-old best. Then you front him with the good news that you have mowed the lawns for him and, holding out your hand, you tell him that will be ten bucks, thanks. Now, because Dad doesn't have the feeling that this is something you are doing for him, he can sense that you are coming from 'what's in it for me'. He's somewhat taken aback.

He thinks to himself, did he have a want or a need? Well, yes, he did, but maybe he could have done it himself. Come inspection time, he can see that the edges haven't been done. In fact, it's not the way that Dad would have done the job at all. Now he thinks to himself, does he value paying ten dollars for the job you have done for him?

This time the answer is definitely *No!* This time you get criticism, ridicule.

'Ten bucks for that job! If I'd done as bad a job of the lawns as you have, my Dad would've laughed, not paid me ten bucks. Do the edges and I'll consider five dollars, maybe.'

Now you have demonstrated your incompetence and this affects your self-esteem. Firstly, you look to justify or rationalise your behaviour, blaming the other person. 'Boy, what a skinflint my Dad is! I was only trying to do what he said I had to do, earn some money! What a meanie.'

Now your self-esteem and energy drops and lowers your awareness even further. This allows you to absolve yourself totally from blame. In fact, you can justify anything if you put your mind to it. So, understand that whenever you hear someone rationalising, justifying or blaming someone else for their misfortunes, they're in the negative cycle of the laws of real value. And the more we blame or justify, the lower our awareness drops so that we can believe what we say, and this low awareness allows us to do more unethical things.

How do you move someone from the negative cycle to the positive cycle? In other words, how would you convince Dad to give you the ten dollars you want to earn? Well, firstly, you begin by coming from the point of view of what's in it for him: you ask him what he wants, what he needs. You keep asking questions to find what it is that he would value getting from you. Then you find ways to give him more of it. This puts you in the positive cycle of the laws of real value.

In the negative cycle, you assumed he would value what you did. In fact, it really wasn't that you had done a shocking job of the lawns, it was just that the edges weren't done as well. He sensed that you were doing it for your own interest and this led him to become very critical of you and reject what you thought was a reasonable job. To find what he would value, you must ask him. All too often, we act on what we think we know. And we're wrong. Even if you're off beam just a little, it will be enough to tip the scales away from you. How many times have you given people what they want, only to find that they don't value what you have done at all? You have been in the negative cycle of the laws of real value.

Real value for employees

I have done this exercise with managers while coaching and have countless examples of how effective this concept is with employees. The simple concept behind motivating employees is to find what they value about where they work, and give them more of it. This is such a simple concept that we wonder why we don't do it. The answer is twofold. We're too busy and we think we already know what they value. In every case, when managers have done this exercise for me in a coaching session, whether with their employees or their senior managers, there have either been surprises or they have been completely wrong in their assumptions. Let's look at an example.

Firstly, understand that whenever you ask people why they work where they do, they will probably automatically answer that they're there for the money. They may not have looked any deeper than that before. If that's the answer you get, roll over it and continue.

A manager I was coaching was horrified at the idea of doing this exercise. He said that his staff were really negative and all he would get would be complaints that he wouldn't be able to handle, or wouldn't want to hear. I explained to him that he was to focus on the positive. If they started to complain, he was to insist that they focus for a moment on what it was that they liked about working there. After all, if it was so bad, why were they still there?

He reluctantly did the exercise and made a stunning discovery. His staff was a small telemarketing and telephone sales team within a large company that was going through enormous change. There was great disruption, leading to disgruntled staff who were focusing on what they were losing in the changes rather than what ultimate rewards the changes might bring in the future.

Without exception, his people told him that they enjoyed being a small team within such a large organisation. The trick is to find what they value and give them more of it. And it's important to note that what they value is usually something intangible. My client's people valued being a small team, therefore he had to find a way to give them a stronger feeling of being a team.

> **The trick is to find what they value and give them more of it.**

He thought about it for a while and then decided to call a weekly meeting with his people and nominated one of them to be the chairperson each meeting. It was their meeting that he just happened to sit in on as one of the team. Then he started to do other spontaneous things to build the team spirit. He sent them a memo to be in the boardroom at 10 o'clock on a Wednesday morning. When they arrived and were seated, somewhat subdued, wondering what was coming, he wheeled in a trolley with coffee and chocolate biscuits to say that they'd been doing such a good job he thought they should have a tea break together. And by this time, he wasn't lying. His team was positive, energetic with high morale. He could scarcely believe that it was the same team as the negative, critical group of a few weeks before.

Real value for the boss

This exercise is as relevant upwards as it is downwards with your staff. Imagine the impact it would have on your relationship with your boss if you knew what he or she valued about you and you were able to give more of it.

Again, don't make any assumptions. I was coaching a manager who said she knew what her boss valued about her, but I encouraged her to do the exercise anyway. Well, she had guessed one out of three. What her boss put at the top of the list was her problem-solving ability. This was something that was so easy for this person to do that she didn't value it herself and couldn't believe that her boss really valued it that much. She wanted to be valued for other things, and spent much of her time giving lip service to what her boss valued and put time and energy into what she herself valued about herself in the hope that she could convert her boss. Perhaps she'll think more on this concept as she enjoys her redundancy.

Creating real value with clients

An advertising representative listened to this concept and decided it sounded easy enough, and she would give it a try. She told me that she tried it on the next client she was seeing for the first time. He was the marketing manager for a chain of retail outlets, and he had called in cold and said he wanted to do an advertising campaign. She had identified what he wanted, a successful advertising campaign, but she still had to identify what it was that he valued. You ask to get the want or need; you keep asking to get the value.

> **You ask to get the want or need; you keep asking to get the value.**

She asked, 'What do you want to achieve with this campaign?'

He didn't even need to think about the answer to that question. 'I want to increase the shop traffic — dramatically.'

45

'Why? What will happen if you do that?'

'Well, we'll make more profit.'

As he had said this without lighting up, she knew that she hadn't found what he valued. So she kept going far beyond what the average salesperson would ask. 'And what would happen then? Why's that important?'

She told me he leaned across the table, and she knew before he said another word that she was going to hear what he valued.

'Because then I'll have shown them that I'm the best damn marketing manager they've ever had in this company!'

Now, whenever she phones him and says, 'I've got this great idea for a campaign that will show you up as a really creative marketing manager', do you think he's going to tell her he's too busy? Of course not. Because he feels she really understands him and is on his side. He'll share his plans with her and they'll have an unusual degree of honesty. They're well on their way to a great relationship. Giving them what they want makes a sale. Giving them what they value creates a loyal relationship.

Giving them what they want makes a sale. Giving them what they value creates a loyal relationship.

Why don't all salespeople use this technique? Well, the incredibly successful ones do, they use it instinctively. Some of the rest will use it when they learn about it, some won't. The ones who won't use it are those who feel that they are being too nosy if they ask a lot of questions. Or they might think that they'll look stupid asking such obvious questions. After all, everybody wants to make more profit, right? Right, but not for the same reasons. And if you don't know what those reasons are, you can't add value. It will take you much longer to create a strong and loyal relationship. And you'll be no more on their side than the next salesperson who comes through their door trying to sell them something.

Understand that by just asking these questions, remembering that you must be coming from the point of view of what's in it for them, you make other people feel valued by you. Nobody is usually that interested in what they're doing. So just going through the process is a relationship-building exercise.

Finding the value gives you an incredibly powerful tool. Using it will mean that you help make their business more efficient or more profitable. We're not talking about manipulation here. We're talking about valuable ongoing relationships with a mutually satisfying exchange.

Real value in relationships

Soula was in a happy, stable relationship but was wise enough to know that you always need to keep working at it. She knew that relationships never automatically keep improving. If it's not growing, it's dying. While it may appear to be stagnant or still, if it's not growing, make no mistake, it's dying. All things go through cycles and relationships are no different. We move closer together and have warm loving times together, then we move away and create distance. It's often at this distance that we become critical of our partner and forget to keep working on the relationship to make sure that we then move into the cycle of moving closer together.

So, when Soula learnt this process, she decided to try it on her relationship. She felt a little stupid because they had been together for more than ten years, but she persisted.

'What is it that you like about our relationship?'

Her partner, Bob, thought that was a bit of a strange question. 'Why do you want to know that for?'

'I want to know that so, once I know what it is, I can give you more of whatever it is. So?'

'Great sex,' he said with a grin.

'Okay, but what else do you like about our relationship? What do you value about it?'

47

Bob was a bit disconcerted; he figured the crack about great sex would put her off. He thought about it for a moment. 'I don't really know. I love you.'

Bob shrugged hoping she'd give up, but Soula just sat there looking at him, waiting. So he thought about it a bit more. 'I'll tell you what I like. I like it on a Sunday afternoon when we take the dog and go for one of our long walks. We talk to each other and it feels as if we really listen to each other. And we don't get any interruptions, like family or phone calls.' He realised that he'd become quite intense and, a little embarrassed, finished by saying, 'Yeah, I really like that.'

Soula remembered all the times when Bob had asked her if she wanted to go for a long walk with the dog and she had put him off. Too busy, too many things to do that seemed more important than walking the dog. But now she realised that there was much more involved than just walking the dog. She knew that she would never again turn him down when he wanted to walk the dog, because she now knew how much that time together added to their relationship. Bob's voice interrupted her thoughts. 'So, what about you?'

'What?'

'What do you value about our relationship?' Bob was a fast learner and he could see what she had just identified.

Soula learnt how difficult it could be on the receiving end of this question. 'To be honest, I haven't thought about it much either.'

'Well, think,' insisted Bob. 'I want to know as well.'

'Well,' Soula searched her memory for warm moments of happiness and struck gold. 'I know what it is. You make me laugh. Your sense of humour always makes me laugh, it lightens me when I get too serious. And I like the way that someone will say something and I look at you and you know exactly what I'm thinking. And we both burst out laughing and no one knows what we're laughing at.'

The result of the question deepened and strengthened the relationship even further.

Remember one last thing, what you value changes. So once you've got it, don't assume that it's always going to be the same, you have to check from time to time to see if it has changed. It's so easy, ask and find

48

what they value — and give them more of it.

Laws of real value in children

This concept works just as effectively with children as adults. I taught it to one of my clients to help him improve his interaction with his staff. He was aware that he wasn't much of a people person and realised that he was the one at fault when his secretary resigned. The coaching worked so well that his secretary withdrew her resignation. Glen was a very practical person, and after seeing the effect of the laws of real value on his secretary and staff, he asked me whether it would work on his son. He had a nine-year-old boy, Tran, and he was concerned about Tran's disruptive behaviour. I encouraged him to give it a try, and this is what he told me happened.

He went into Tran's bedroom one night just before lights out and asked him what Tran wanted from him as a father. His son asked him why he was asking, and Glen told him that he wanted to make sure that he was giving Tran everything he could that was important to him. Tran told him that he'd like to spend more time with him. Glen, being the practical person that he is, asked what would they do with this time they had together. Tran sat up in bed with an excited expression on his face (the clue to indicate that Glen had got to what Tran would value) and made a few suggestions, go to the zoo or a game of football together. But, Tran added, it would have to be just the two of them, no one else around. Glen fetched his diary and booked in some time for the two of them to spend together, and started thinking of how he was going to explain this to his daughter.

I saw Glen two weeks later and he told me the change in his son's behaviour had been nothing short of astounding. Now that Tran is getting the attention he values, he has dropped the demanding behaviour that got him the substitute attention.

Summary

The laws of real value work equally well with clients, employees and family and friends. The secret of the laws of real value is that the people you are dealing with feel valued.

The rules for establishing this are simple:

- Come from the point of view of what's in it for them, not what's in it for you.
- Ask them what they want or need.
- Keep asking them what they want or need until you get to what they value. They will light up or get excited when they tell you about it. You can check to see if you've got it by asking, 'Is that important to you?' If they say, 'Not really', or aren't hugely enthusiastic, you haven't got it. Keep asking. 'What would happen if you got (the want)?'
- Give them more of what they value.
- Check occasionally to see if what they value has changed.

If you are on the negative cycle of the laws of real value, you have come from the point of view of what's in it for you. People will pick up on this, and will not feel valued.

- Go back and begin again, this time from the point of view of what's in it for them.
- Find out what they value and give them more of it.

- Knowing what people want isn't enough. You have to give them more of what they value.

4 DO THEY FEEL LISTENED TO?

Let's see if you can relate to this scenario. You work for a company with a department of ten people reporting to you. Michelle works for you and, while she is a capable person, she is operating a system she is new to. You used the system at the last company you worked for.

Michelle comes to you with a problem she is having with the system. She is halfway through telling you about it when you recognise the problem as similar to the one you had when you first started operating the system. You break in and tell her what to try, and go back to your work. The next morning Michelle is back again. This time, you listen to what she says, but something she says triggers you off, and while she continues to tell you about this new problem you're thinking about whether the new solution you've thought of will work or not. Having thought it through, you tell her what to do and away she goes. You notice she's looking a bit down and ask her if she's okay. She says that the whole system is getting her down, but you reassure her and tell her that it will be fine once she's got the hang of it.

The next day, she's back again. This time you can see that she's angry. You ask her what the matter is and she tells you that the system is hopeless, it isn't compatible with how things are done around here and it's not working for any of the departments. Everyone is having major problems with it. You are stunned. This is the first you knew about there being widespread problems. Michelle mutters that if only you'd just listen for a change, maybe you'd find out.

You are shocked. She thinks you don't listen. And yet you had listened to her and you had given her solutions that worked, you might add. How can she accuse you of not listening?

Have you ever been accused of not listening? At the time, you probably denied it vehemently. You heard every word! And solved the problem.

One of the biggest obstacles in communication is that we focus on what other people are saying, not on what they are attempting to communicate. So, when people accuse you of not listening, they may actually mean that they simply don't feel listened to. This has a vastly different meaning. You may be listening intently and they can still not feel listened to. So, how do you go about making them feel listened to? You're always listening, so it's something you're already doing! No, it's something you're not doing. Confused? Good.

> **One of the biggest obstacles in communication is that we focus on what other people are saying, not on what they are attempting to communicate.**

Most of the time when we are listening to people, we are either:
- waiting to say something,
- trying to relate to what they are saying to our own lives, or
- looking for solutions.

Surprisingly, there are situations where none of these is an appropriate way of listening.

If you are waiting to have your say, your focus is on yourself and what you are going to say next. You wait for the other person to stop to take a breath, and you're in. This isn't listening. It's not even pretending to listen. It's more like having a captive audience. Pity the poor person who made the mistake of starting up a conversation with you. This happens all the time in social situations; it's not as common in a business situation.

> **You wait for the other person to stop to take a breath, and you're in. This isn't listening.**

Often we listen to people only until we can relate what they are saying to our own lives. We filter everything that is said to us.

'I'm having real trouble with my son.'

'Really? What's the problem?'

'Well, most of the time he won't even talk to me, and when he does, he's so cheeky and smart-mouthed, I just get angry with him. We seem to be yelling at each other all the time. I'm worried he wants to leave home but I don't know how to change our relationship.'

'I know exactly what you mean. When my daughter was young...' and away you go, telling your friend all about when you had a similar problem, what it was like for you and how you did or didn't solve it. So now your friend is sitting listening to your past problems and wondering what this has got to do with his son. He may perceive that the circumstances are totally different, but you are rattling on regardless. You're like the horse who's lost its rider but finishes the race regardless. Hey, but you feel better now because you shared your problem. But chances are, the other person doesn't feel as if you have listened to him. And he probably feels as if you don't understand how it is for him. So he withdraws. Later, if you have a disagreement with him, he will probably accuse you of never listening and you will be stunned. When have you not listened to him?

What you are doing in this situation is reading your own biography into the other person's life. As soon as you can relate to what they're saying, you stop listening and go into your own story.

> **As soon as you can relate to what they're saying, you stop listening and go into your own story.**

We also make the mistake of projecting our intentions onto the other person's behaviour. He doesn't have to explain how he feels, we already know. We know because we remember how we felt. Right? Wrong. There may be added circumstances around this situation which you're not yet aware of. But understand that the minute we go into our own autobiography, the other person shuts down.

He isn't going to struggle upstream against the current of your experience. He'll just let you talk and feel resentful that you don't understand and don't listen to him.

Looking for solutions is one of the most common reasons managers have for not listening. You wait until you have heard enough to identify the problem and then you start working at a solution. While you are working at a solution, you are not listening.

This is particularly common with male managers. If someone is telling them a problem, they want to find a solution. And fast. You see, most men are fix-it seekers and problem solvers. If there's a problem, they like to find a solution. (By now, the men will be asking, what else would you do if someone's asking for help with a problem?)

> **While you are working at a solution, you are not listening.**

So, if you go to a man with a problem, more than likely he will tell you how to fix it and send you on your way. The only problem is that the way he would fix it and handle it may not be a way you'd feel comfortable with. Or, what you were saying to him hasn't actually got to the heart of the problem. Either you don't yet know what the real problem is, or you know what it is but you're not going to share it with Mr Know-how-to-fix-everything because he wouldn't understand. Let me explain, firstly from the recipient's point of view.

'I've been looking at your sales figures and they're not good. What do you think you're doing wrong?'

Now you know he has good intentions and you would like to improve, so you say what you think you're weak at.

'Well, I'm making the calls and I get on really well with my clients. I mean, I know they like me, and trust me, too.'

'I'm sure they do. But you're just not getting the sales from them.

What's missing?'

'I'm probably not closing as strongly as I should, I suppose.'

'Yes, that's what I suspected. Well, let me tell you how to do it.' And away he goes, telling you how he used to close the sale when he was on the road. But, in your eyes, he's a hard person, whereas you really care about your clients. If they say they've already spent their budget, you're not going to push them. If they say they only use your competitors, you're not going to argue with them.

So you listen to him, you go along with what he's saying and carry on doing things the way you always have. Result, nothing changes. You leave the meeting feeling frustrated and wondering if a career in selling really is for you. And you are left with the impression of how wonderful the manager thinks he is at selling. He can probably close every sale, and that thought makes you feel even more inadequate.

The manager thinks he did a good job in the meeting. He addressed the problem, he educated and he motivated. But you left feeling frustrated and demotivated. Eventually, the manager will be puzzling over why nothing has changed.

If the manager was really listening to you, the conversation would have gone something like this.

'But you're just not getting the sales from them. What's missing?

'I'm probably not closing as strongly as I should, I suppose.'

'Why do you think that is?'

'Well, I don't like to push them, I like to leave them to make their decision and call them back.'

'I see, and what else stops you from closing?'

'Well, some of them have spent their budget, others just aren't interested.'

In a perfect world, this manager would now give you training on handling objections and address the Nice Guy in you. He would give you techniques for helping your clients make a decision. You would leave this meeting feeling as if he really understood and listened to you. He cared about what happened to you and gave you some tools and techniques to try. Notice that throughout the whole meeting his focus was on you. Can you see that the first scenario is completely autobiographical? The manager's focus was on himself and how he would close. In other words, he flicked back through his life, to see if he had had a similar problem and remembered how he solved it. 'I know exactly what you're saying and why you're hesitating.' Then he shared.

What needs to happen is for you to be able to explain fully the problem as you see it, with all your concerns, so that the manager can help you find a solution you will find acceptable. So, how can the manager help this happen?

Rules for the game of listening

Because our culture is so sports-oriented, let's make it a game. Let me explain the rules for the game of listening. Firstly, you ask questions — open questions, not closed questions, questions designed to get the other person talking and talking freely.

- Don't ask questions that will give you the answer you knew they would give.
- Don't ask questions that will reveal to them that you know what the problem is when they can't see it.
- Don't ask closed questions.

Closed questions get a yes, no, or one-word answer. Closed questions give you specific information. We use them to get information at the end of the sale, or for identifying exactly what a problem might be. 'Would you like blue or red?' 'Exactly when did the light come on?' 'How long have you been waiting?'

Don't underestimate how hard a habit this is to break. And if you want to be good at building relationships with your people and clients, you'd better learn how to stop asking closed questions, fast. Closed questions are used to confirm and control the conversation. If you're controlling the conversation, will they feel as if you're listening to them? No, they won't. They'll feel as if you already know the answers, but they may still feel that you don't really understand their situation. The bottom line is that closed questions shut the other person down. After all, after they have answered your question, there's not much left to say. It is one of the reasons that new salespeople sound as if they are grilling the client; they are asking closed question after closed question and there's no normal conversation flow.

Open questions get the other person talking. If you know how to do this well, your next problem may be how to get people to stop talking, even if you have just met them for the first time. I've seen open questions used well with a new client. One open question about her business and the rep just sat and listened for the next twenty minutes.

In a management situation, open questions involve the other person in thinking through the problem and possible solutions. Open questions ask what and why; they say tell me about... And your role is to listen.

- Don't evaluate the information. That is, don't agree or disagree. Even sympathy is a form of agreeing.
- Don't dig. This is using your own experience and background to dig for information so you can relate to it.
- Don't give any advice at this stage.
- Don't interpret what the other person is saying or try to explain the other person's behaviour or motives using your own experience.

This removes just about all the strategies most of us have for listening. So what on earth do you do?

Genuine listening

Before you can offer advice or solutions, you need to understand the other person's problem, and not by working out how you would handle it if it was your problem. You need to understand the problem from the other person's point of view. That's why the highest form of listening is called empathetic listening. The power of empathy is to walk in other people's shoes and feel their feelings. And if you've ever been accused of not listening, this is a skill you have yet to develop.

> **You need to understand the problem from the other person's point of view.**

You need to understand three things.
- How do they feel about the problem?
- Why is it worrying them so much?
- What is stopping them from doing something about it?

When you understand how they feel about the problem, why it is worrying them and what is stopping them from doing something about it, you'll be starting to appreciate their problem. But understand that these questions are only for your guidance — if you actually ask them, you will be probing.

So, how do you get this information? Most people won't reveal too much for fear of appearing stupid or weak, or any number of other false impressions they think they're going to leave with you. They feel that they've got a lot to lose, maybe even their job, if they are honest and open with you. They have to feel safe and they have to feel that you are really interested. So, you have to give them time to peel the onion layer by layer until they get to the heart of the problem. They need room to move, to get to the real problem in their own time.

You may already be feeling a little uneasy. You see, when you learn and apply this technique, you know one thing for sure, you're going to learn what the real underlying problem is. This means that somehow you're going to have to contribute to solving it. And the last thing we all need is another problem, right? Right. So why go looking for more problems when we could give them a solution to the obvious one and send them on their way? It's a bit like looking for cancer. What happens if you find it? It's not really something you want to look for, and you definitely don't want to find it.

But the fact is, when there are problems that people won't talk to you about, it will affect their performance and you won't know how to fix it. Genuine listening is a vital skill for managers. Many managers with good people handling skills will do this instinctively, sometimes almost by accident. They don't know what they do, they just know that they can help people open up to them and confide in them. Because they aren't consciously aware of how they do this, they will be unlikely to be as successful at it with their families.

> **Genuine listening is a vital skill for managers.**

This technique can be learned. But don't think for a minute that it's easy to develop these kinds of listening skills. It's not, it's difficult to overcome the urge to probe and interpret. But you'll be amazed at how much people will open up to you if you practise. If you are a manager, you'll become a coach, a counsellor and a mentor in the true sense of the words. Imagine how motivating that is for the person who works for you. To be listened to and understood is one of the most powerfully affirming experiences we can have. It creates incredibly loyal staff because your people feel that you are perceptive, a good listener and you really care about them.

> **To be listened to and understood is one of the most powerfully affirming experiences we can have.**

Risks in genuine listening

There is risk attached to this kind of listening. You will feel vulnerable because you are opening yourself up to be influenced. This takes a sense of security in your own self and in your own judgement. But make no mistake: the rewards in openness, honesty and a strong relationship through this type of listening are immense.

> **You will feel vulnerable because you are opening yourself up to be influenced.**

Another feeling you may come up against is one that a young manager fed back to me when he tried this technique. He asked me, 'But while I'm listening, what do I *do*? I feel as if I'm not *doing* anything.' He was almost compulsively directed to finding solutions. And so it is with some people; they feel they must offer a solution. Just sitting there and listening feels to them as if they are not contributing to the conversation. They feel they are not helping.

So, expect some uncomfortable feelings to kick in when you first start practising this technique. Acknowledge them and continue. And I must say once again, this will be a challenging technique for many men to learn. Men can be good listeners, but it can be difficult for very action-oriented men not to rush in and fix things with good advice. Believe me, the good intention will not be welcomed by people who believe that you're not listening to them.

Listen with your eyes

The heart of the technique of genuine listening is to listen with your eyes. To listen with your eyes means that you don't respond to what people are saying, you respond to what you can see and you feed that back to them. Do they look frustrated, embarrassed or uncomfortable? When you identify what you can see, feed that back to them rather than commenting on what they're saying. Let's take the example of the rep who's not closing the sale.

> **The heart of the technique of genuine listening is to listen with your eyes.**

'Well, I know I'm making the calls and I get on really well with my clients. I mean, I know they like me and trust me, too.'

'I'm sure they do. But you're just not getting the sales from them. Can you tell me why?'

'I'm probably not closing as strongly as I should, I suppose.'

'You look a little uncomfortable when we talk about closing the sale.' Notice no agreement or disagreement, no judgement, just a feeding back of what you see.

'Well, I've got to admit, it's probably the part of the sale I feel the least comfortable about.'

At this stage, if you were to say, 'Tell me why you don't like closing,' you would be probing. Probing is against the rules. Probing means that you are looking for solutions and this means that you're not listening.

'Well, I mean, I know you're meant to close, but it's not always the right thing to do.'

'You look as if you really don't like closing the sale.'

'Well, you can't always, can you?'

'The thought of closing the sale upsets you a bit at times?' You're not judging in any way, you're simply giving the rep room to move so that he can keep going. This will lead to the heart of the problem.

'Yes, it does, I guess. I mean, when they say that they want time to think about it, I'm not going to push and force the issue. And if they've used their budget, what's the point of being pushy? You're better off keeping the good relationship with them and perhaps getting the order next year before they've used their budget. Do you know what I mean?'

'I think so. You're saying that when you close the sale, you feel as if you're being pushy.'

'Exactly! And I'm good at creating relationships with my clients, I'm not going to threaten that because some sales manual says that you've got to close every sale.'

Now what do you know about the problem? Firstly, the rep has an attitude towards closing the sale that isn't going to change no matter how many solutions you come up with. He doesn't know the difference between real and false objections and, as a person who values making relationships so highly, he'll do nothing which in his eyes, may threaten that relationship. You can tell him what works, but if he doesn't feel good about it, he won't do it.

In my experience, this kind of person can make a great salesperson because of his focus on the client. He builds long-term trusting relationships where he becomes an adviser to the client. But he will only be successful in the eyes of his employer if his attitude towards closing can be addressed. Getting him to identify this as the problem is the first step. If he feels that you understand both him and his clients, he'll be more open to continuing this discussion towards a solution. In other words, this will now become a journey of exploration and discovery together.

Listening to women
Generally speaking, men and women handle problems differently and need to be listened to differently. When a man has a problem, he usually contracts until he is focused completely on the problem and only that problem. He will think it through, and if he can't solve it, he will go to someone to talk about it. When a man talks about a problem, he is usually giving the other person permission to help solve it. So he is looking for a Mr Fix-it. If he doesn't talk about his problem, and you offer him solutions, he will think that you consider him to be inadequate in some way.

> **When a man talks about a problem, he is usually giving the other person permission to help solve it.**

When a woman has a problem she doesn't usually contract and focus on that one problem. She usually does the opposite to a man and expands to take in all her problems in addition to the one she's worried about. She gets herself into a huge emotional turmoil, which increases the stress she feels about the original problem. Rather than get solutions, a woman needs to talk about how the problem makes her feel. As she talks about it, her stress levels will lower and she will then be ready for solutions. Jump in too early with solutions at your peril! Not only will she resent it, she will accuse you of not listening to her.

> **Rather than get solutions, a woman needs to talk about how the problem makes her feel.**

This one aspect of communication is probably at the heart of most domestic dissatisfactions between men and women. And it lies at the heart of the disrespect that many women employees have for new male managers. When new, the manager will try to offer solutions because he wants to help people. And the only way he knows how to help is to solve problems. So he goes heavily into solutions and finds that the women in his team either resent his help or blatantly ignore him and his solutions. Tough isn't it? Can you see how good intentions without understanding the other person can really work against you?

Here is one last example to demonstrate how important it is that the person feels listened to. I was called in to work with a young woman who was in a sales position. The manager explained to me that she was a valuable member of the team, she was good at her job and they would like to keep her if they possibly could. Some of her behaviour was causing problems and she had received her second warning letter. Nothing had changed. It looked as if they were going to have to give her the third letter and lose her. Was there any way in which I could work with her to change her behaviour so they could keep her on?

The manager explained that the sales manager had had two interviews with her, the general manager had had three interviews with her, two at work and one more casually over a cup of coffee. She'd had an interview after each letter, and they'd not been able to make a difference.

I met with her and found her eager to stay with the company. I used open questions, made no assumptions about her behaviour, fed back to her what I could see she was feeling rather than reacting to what she was saying, and suddenly she burst into tears. She apologised, but explained that she was so relieved that someone was finally listening to her. Seven interviews she'd had. Seven times they had attempted to communicate with her. They had wanted her to stay and she had wanted to stay, but they hadn't been able to address the problem. Seven meetings and she said I was the first person who had really listened to her. Think about it. Do your people feel listened to? And how do you know?

Managers listening to teams

One of the more serious challenges I have faced in my career was the time I was created classified advertising manager of two daily newspapers. My brief was to increase the classified ads, but I didn't have any reps actively selling classifieds. In fact, the only people who were 'selling', were the women in the phone room. And I had only two small problems with training them. Their union had declared that because they keyed straight into the system, they were not eligible for sales training. They were printers. And a bloody-minded union it was in those days, too! In fact, they would sit and knit between incoming calls. They would neither increase the wording of the ads nor did they care too much whether they were accurate.

The second problem was that they weren't speaking to each other! I remember standing and watching them, knitting away between calls, asking someone across the room to pass on a message to the person sitting next to them. They were in such discord that they would not turn their heads and speak to the person next to them. They would call across the room to the person they were currently speaking to and ask them to pass the message back across the room to the person sitting right next to them! This was a total breakdown of communication.

My job was to get them to pull together as a team and teach them basic sales skills. I decided to use a timeless training tool, a cask of wine. I called a meeting at the end of the day to discuss some of the problems we'd been having and, yes, I paid them overtime. As I was a new manager, I put to them, they were more likely to have the solutions to some of the systems that were causing us problems.

A glass or two into the session and I was stunned with some of the solutions they had come up with. And their enthusiasm and their energy had risen. Believe me, it had very little to do with the wine. I threw another problem onto the table, a real curly one. This one was an age-old friend that no one in the country had found a solution to. I sat back and watched. They discussed it among themselves and asked me to leave it with them because they had some ideas but needed to really spend some time on it.

In the middle of this session, we did some sales training. We put together some questions for them to ask when an ad came in. These were questions that would get more information from the advertiser for the reader, and, incidentally, make the ad a little longer. Then we went back to solving more problems. First sales training session accomplished!

When I was satisfied that they were all speaking to each other again, I wound the meeting up. They hadn't finished, and neither was the wine. I wound it up three times before I could get them out the door. They wandered out, still discussing the issues, completely forgetting that when they had walked into the room, they hadn't been speaking to each other.

At the time, I didn't really know what it was that had worked. I now know that there were several issues that affected them.

The first thing was that this team hadn't been managed. I'm amazed at the number of companies that just expect a team to function. Whenever I'm called into a company where there's a problem within the sales team, I also check out the manager. Teams need either strong guidelines for managing themselves or a firm manager. Without this in place, the behaviour drops to the lowest common denominator. And once this happens, of course, the good people leave, and it gets worse. If you have a problem within your team and you're pointing the finger at behaviour you would like changed, look at the hand you are pointing with and see how many fingers are pointing back at you. I believe that fifty per cent of problems within a team are management problems, or, more likely, lack of management.

> **Teams need either strong guidelines for managing themselves or a firm manager.**

The second thing was that once the meeting began they felt involved and listened to. They had the opportunity to contribute. They had many solutions to problems that management had been struggling with for months, but no one had asked them and they had resented it. So, not only had they not offered solutions, they had sneered at management's attempts to make them more efficient. I treated them as intelligent adults and they responded as intelligent adults. It's our own attitudes that dictate how we treat our staff and how we treat people often determines how they will respond and behave. And never underestimate the impact of being listened to.

Summary

Focus on what people are attempting to communicate, not what they are saying.

- If you are waiting to say something, or if you are relating what other people are saying to your own life, or if you are looking for solutions, you are not listening.
- Understand the problem from the point of view of the person with the problem.
- Follow the rules of the game of listening:
    - Ask open questions, not closed questions.
    - Do not evaluate the information.
    - Do not dig for information.
    - Do not give any advice (at this stage).
    - Do not interpret.
- Genuine listening requires that you respond to what you can see, not what you can hear, and feed that back to the person you are listening to. This is listening with your eyes.
- Generally speaking, listening to men is different from listening to women. A man usually talks about a problem because he wants a solution. A woman usually talks about a problem because she wants to express how she feels about it. Then she will be prepared to listen to a solution.
- Teams given the opportunity to contribute will find solutions to problems that management can struggle with for months.
- Teams given the opportunity to contribute won't sabotage the efforts of management to create change or make improvements.

5 TRIGGERING OTHER PEOPLE

Listening to people is a powerful management tool. But, having read the previous chapter, you may have tried genuine listening and found that there are one or two people in your company with whom it didn't work. Regardless of what you do or how you do it, you always end up butting heads, frustrated with each other. With the best of intentions, you decide that this time you will keep calm, you won't get frustrated or annoyed. You will talk it over quietly together, and he or she will understand your point of view. Right? Wrong. Every time you talk to this person, you end up with the same result and the same feeling of intense frustration.

Managers are encouraged to be strong leaders. This means that they make things happen. They can see the big picture and take responsibility for making it happen. These are all good qualities, ones that companies value highly. Therefore, the manager instinctively recognises leadership as a successful action. This is where the trouble starts.

Cause and effect

Leaders cause things to happen. And when people cause things to happen, they feel in control. I describe people like this as being 'cause'. When you are cause, others will feel the effect of you and won't always like it. It can be a very uncomfortable place to be, especially for men. I call this being 'at-the-effect'. If you feel at-the-effect of a person, you can feel out of control. Being at-the-effect of someone can make you feel like a subordinate. And if you also like to feel in control, you will strongly resist feeling like a subordinate. You may take it from managers senior to you, but you will not allow one of your fellow managers to make you feel subordinate to them.

When you are in cause, it may not be your intention to make others feel at-the-effect, but that's the impact you will have. If you don't want people to be aggressive, defensive or resentful, you will have to learn to handle them by being at-the-effect, instead of being cause. That is, of course, unless you don't care about the effect you have on them, but just want them to do what you want done.

> **If you don't want people to be aggressive, defensive or resentful, you will have to learn to handle them by being at-the-effect, instead of being cause.**

For example, a conversation between you and another manager where you are being cause, might go like this. You are sitting at your desk going over some figures when the other manager enters and stands just inside the doorway. She is obviously annoyed.

'Look, we've got to do something about this system of monitoring the orders. My people are wasting too much time backtracking and trying to find out where the order is in the system.'

'I've told you that we can't change the system to suit you, you'll just have to work with it. It's not my problem.'

The other manager turns and leaves the office, seething with rage and frustration. She wants to work this problem through with you but your attitude always rubs her up the wrong way.

You feel resentment at her demands. You have no intention of spending time trying to work out another system for someone who is only interested in her own department. You feel as if she is putting your department in the wrong.

Both of you resent the fact that you can't work together as a team and blame one another for this failure. Both of you think that it is the other who is making it difficult because both of you intend to co-operate until the other one speaks. If the other manager was aware of the idea of cause, she would handle this meeting quite differently. She would consciously put herself at-the-effect and allow you to be cause and to be in control of the meeting. Now this can be a difficult thing to do for someone who is cause, until she gets to see the results.

The other manager walks into your office, and hesitates. 'Do you have a minute? I'd like to talk to you.'

You look up, mentally taking a deep breath. 'Sure.' Never let it be said that you could be accused of causing a problem. You are always ready to listen — unlike other people you could mention.

She comes in and sits down in the chair across the desk. 'You know we've been having problems with the tracking of the orders.'

You nod, and wait. So far so good.

'Well, I'm at my wits' end. I just don't know what to do about it, and I wondered if you had any ideas.'

Once over the shock, you put down the printouts you were going to bury yourself in to get rid of the other manager, and lean back in your chair. She continues. 'I was thinking about it the other day, and I wondered if there was a way in which we could connect the orders before they entered the system.'

If the other manager stays at-the-effect, you will seriously consider her suggestion even though you had thought of it earlier and rejected the idea. But now that she's got you listening and co-operating, together you can come up with some alternatives. The instant the other manager goes back into cause, you will withdraw and become very negative about her and her department again.

This is a simple concept that explains many clashes, especially those between department managers. Managers are meant to be in control so they feel uncomfortable when another manager makes them feel at-the-effect. They will lock into being cause and push back. Regardless of good intentions, they will not work well together.

If you are strong cause you will have a range of people responding to you in a range of ways. They will be defensive in the extreme at the drop of a hat, they will be aggressive and will push back. If ever you have found yourself taking a step back in surprise and wondering where that anger or frustration came from in the other person, know that you were in cause. They felt at-the-effect and didn't like it at all. Especially if they are used to feeling cause themselves.

Another time when being cause gets in the way, is in a selling situation. I remember going to see a very senior manager of a large corporation. After shaking hands and getting settled, he crossed his arms, crossed his legs, and said, 'Right. You've got five minutes.' Now that's heavy cause!

If I had gone in as heavy cause and started selling enthusiastically, he would have given me my five minutes and then shown me the door. That's a sure fire way to demonstrate to the other person that you have control of the situation. You kick them out. So, I deliberately sat back in my chair and gave a quick summary of why I had gone to see him, with a big benefit in it for him of why he should listen to me further, of course. Then, at my best at-the-effect behaviour, I asked him, 'So do you want to hear more?' and waited for his answer. He grinned and said, 'You've got a little more time. Keep going.' But he uncrossed his arms and sat back in his chair. In other words, he clearly felt he was in control, and did not feel threatened or sold to by me, so he could afford to relax. Ultimately, we worked on a project together, but I was always aware that he was heavy cause. I took care never to be heavy cause with him, and we worked well together.

Ego states

As a manager, it is your job to ensure that your people perform. You probably spend a lot of your time working on strategies to make that happen. You care about them and want them to succeed. But handling people, even with the best of intentions, has its pitfalls. Especially for new managers or supervisors.

This is how a meeting may go between you, the manager, and one of your salespeople.

'I wanted to have a word with you on how you're going. I'm worried, your figures aren't looking good this month. What's happening?'

'Look, I know I lost the plot there for a while, but I'm back on track now. If everybody will just leave me alone, I can get on with my job.'

Great. Now how do you feel? Frustrated, a little angry because all you were doing was trying to help and he has rejected that help well and truly. What's wrong with him? I mean, you've been out there in the marketplace, you know what it's like. You want to help him, you know you can help him and he's acting just like your rebellious teenage son. And that's the problem. According to Eric Berne, when you talk to people you operate from one of three ego states — Parent, Adult or Child — and the other person responds from the complementary ego state.

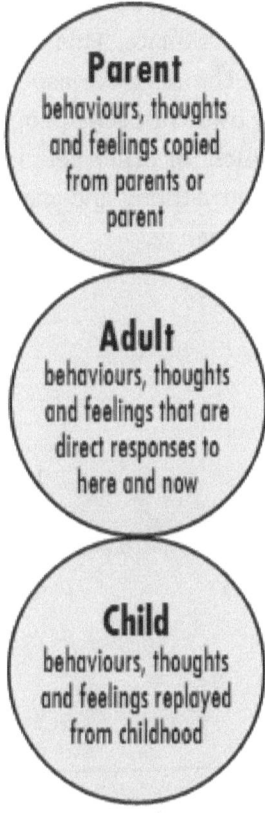

Ego states

The Parent ego state

When you operate from the Parent ego state, you provide and enforce conduct, setting the standards and limits. This ego state is divided into two, the Nurturing Parent and the Controlling or Critical Parent. If you look after and protect your staff, you will Ego states Parent behaviours, thoughts and feelings copied from parents or parent Adult behaviours, thoughts and feelings that are direct responses to here and now Child behaviours, thoughts and feelings replayed from childhood tend to address them from the Parent ego state. Managers often speak to their staff from the Nurturing Parent ego state, which is concerned, understanding and supportive. This is a trap that most eager new managers often fall into. A person in this ego state is saying, 'Let me help you', and is caring and affectionate. This can be very supportive in the appropriate situation, but the negative aspects of the Nurturing Parent ego state take away the power of other people by being over-solicitous. This person will do too much for other people and not demand that they take responsibility for their actions and make a change. In this type of relationship, there is no exchange.

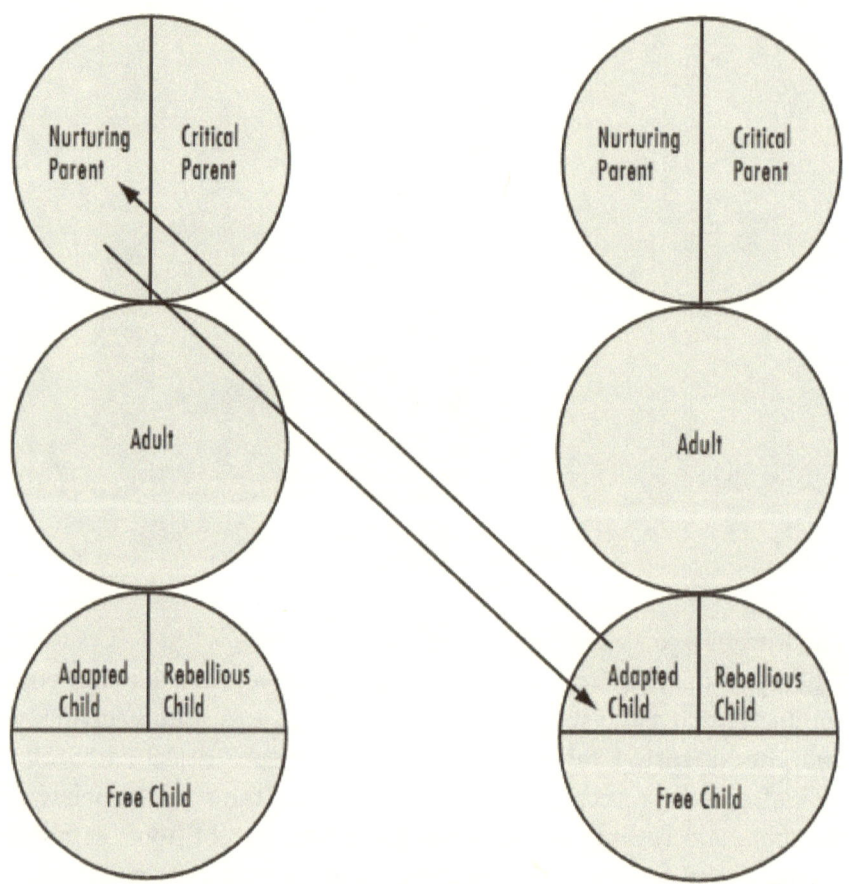

Complementary transaction that doesn't solve problems

One person is simply telling another and supporting the other, and the other is listening and being supported. It might sound like one person has got the other person to take responsibility, but, in reality, nothing changes.

If you speak to one of your staff in the Nurturing Parent ego state and you don't get the change you are looking for, then you will probably switch into the Controlling or Critical Parent ego state. Now you will become critical and preaching, a little bossy and condescending. You'll frown more, have an accusing gaze, and come across as judging and authoritarian. Stop and think for a moment what kind of response you're likely to get when you're operating from this ego state.

If you are in the Parent ego state, you are not just acting in a way that is generally parental. You are reproducing your parents' total behaviour, including their inhibitions, their reasoning, their impulses and their emotions. And remember how you felt when they tried to tell you what to do?

If you are in the Parent ego state, then the other person will answer you from the complementary ego state of the Child.

A clue as to whether or not you're operating from the Parent ego state is to notice if you are saying 'you' a lot during the conversation. 'You should...', 'You don't...', 'You never...', and so on.

There are times when the Parent ego state is appropriate and nurturing, even healing for the other person. The Controlling Parent teaches a child how to cross the road safely, demands that the child stay away from hot stoves and heaters. Both ego states have a valuable role to play in dealings with others. It's only when you're not getting the desired result that you need to check consciously which ego state you're in.

The Child ego state

The Child ego state contains the Adapted Child, the Rebellious Child and the natural Free Child.

The Adapted Child is one of compliance and subservience; in this state, people do as they have been asked. They can be polite, eager to please and eager to learn, but they can also be demanding, fearful and credulous. The body language of people in the Adapted Child ego state includes smiling coyly, pouting or eyes lowered with fluttering eyelashes. Get the picture? You may be thinking that it's a good thing. These are the children who will not cross the road until they have looked both ways, who are obedient and do as they are told. Wouldn't it be a dream come true to have staff who do as they're told? That is very often the problem!

They simply do as they're told and when you start wanting them to show some initiative, they keep coming back to you to find out what they should be doing. You want them to think for themselves, but you always seem to have to make their decisions for them. Unfortunately, you're still behaving in a way that puts them in the Child ego state, so they will continue to wait to be told what to do.

When people are in the Child ego state, they do not simply be- have in a childlike manner, they reproduce behaviours from their own childhood, along with their experiences and very magnified feelings that aren't appropriate to the situation.

The Rebellious Child ego state is exactly what it sounds like. People in this state are angry, resentful and out to prove you wrong. How much progress do you think you will make if you're in Parent ego state and the other person is in Rebellious Child? Not much, I can assure you. And there will be lots of emotion on both sides that will get in the way. How do you solve a problem together if you're feeling frustrated and impatient and the other person is feeling resentful? To get a person to take responsibility and to change, you need a commitment from the Adult, not a promise from the Child — 'I'll try'. The trap here is that salespeople operate much of the time from the Child ego state. This is the area of high energy where there is a strong sense of fun and playfulness. Therefore, it's twice as likely that, as their sales manager, you will be pulled into the Parent ego state.

> **To get a person to take responsibility and change, you need a commitment from the Adult, not a promise from the Child—'I'll try'.**

Some people can trigger you more easily than others into another ego state. With my eldest daughter, I'm easily able to stay out of the Parent ego state and remain in the Adult ego state. But my youngest daughter can kick me into the Nurturing Parent state with just a look. One of her biggest criticisms of our relationship is that I continue to treat her as a teenager. This is a sure indication that I operate from the Parent ego state with her.

The third child ego state is the natural Free Child. This a part of the Child ego state that is uninhibited and has high energy and creativity. A huge sense of fun is usually present when your Free Child responds to another Free Child. But as I don't perceive this ego state to be much of a problem in the breakdown of communication between staff and management, we've only touched on it to let you know that it exists.

The Adult ego state

When you operate from Adult ego state, you are even, measured and calm. You evaluate the facts in a dispassionate and controlled manner. You are objective, unbiased, rational and consistent. You respond to the here-and-now in an appropriate manner as a grown-up. The Adult ego state leads to problem solving.

> **The Adult ego state leads to problem-solving.**

If you find yourself using 'I' a lot in a conversation, this can indicate that you are talking from the Adult ego state.

'I wanted to have a word with you on how you're going. I am concerned that your figures aren't looking promising for this month. I know if you're on track you're usually close to budget at this time of the month. What's happening?'

'Look, I know I lost the plot there for a while, but I'm back on track now. If everybody will just leave me alone, I can get on with my job.'

'So what knocked you off track?' Notice no reaction — calm, measured and interested.

'I don't know, I just seemed to lose it for a while, that's all.' He's still in Child ego state.

'So what is it that you're doing differently now which leads you to believe you're on track again?'

'I'm cold calling regularly again. And I sat down yesterday and started my planning again. I'd dropped that as well.' Now he's in Adult.

'What can you use as a measurement to tell you if you're going off track again?'

'I guess my cold calling is a good indication of where I'm at. If I drop it altogether, then that tells me I'm losing the plot. By the way, I've got this client I wanted to ask you about.'

The two of them can now discuss any subject and both will listen to the other dispassionately without resentment or condescending behaviour getting in the road. Unless one of them kicks back into Parent or Child, to which the other person will react by kicking into the complementary role.

Successful communication

We operate from the complementary ego state to the one that the other person is operating from because it feels then as if the communication is successful. If someone is talking to you from the Adult ego state, it will feel most comfortable and natural to you to answer from your Adult ego state. This is a complementary transaction. A complementary transaction will continue for as long as you choose to keep it going.

In other words, if you are operating from the Parent ego state and the other person is responding from the Rebellious Child, even though you know the communication isn't going anywhere, you will continue operating from those two ego states. You can break off the conversation, but, as soon as you meet again, you will automatically both return to those two ego states. One of you needs to change ego states, and because you're the one trying to change the communication, you need to do it.

Commitment to change can only come from the Adult ego state. The Child ego state will wish, hope and promise, but you know how much the promise from a child can mean. Anything that stops them means they can't keep that promise and it's not their fault. So, if you think about it, you have to be in Adult ego state to get a commitment to change from the other person.

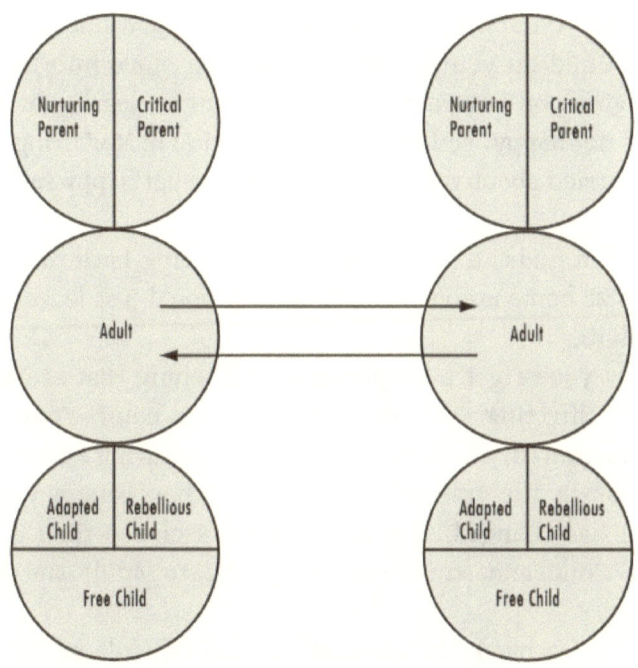

Complementary transaction that solves problems

If you are trying to support and look after them, you will be coming from Nurturing Parent and the other person will automatically pop into Child.

If you go into the Nurturing Parent ego state and the other person doesn't do what you want, usually the next step is to go into Controlling or Critical Parent. You won't be able to help yourself because the emotional reaction will be so strong. So, if you have someone who is operating from Rebellious Child and you go into Controlling Parent, the results would be disastrous and entirely predictable: two angry resentful people who are seething with emotion and not listening to each other. You would have open hostility on your hands and not understand why. This is exactly what happens with your teenagers and often with your staff, too. Behind it all is the tragedy of good intentions.

Blocking or crossing the transaction

If you realise you are in Nurturing Parent and you find yourself with a Rebellious Child on your hands, you need to move into the Adult ego state. Imagine you have a staff member who is clearly not performing well and is not happy. You begin the interaction in Nurturing Parent.

'I'm worried about you, you're not your usual happy self. What's the problem?'

'Look, I'm under a lot of pressure. I'm going hard to reach budget and things at home aren't going so well. If you'd just leave me alone to get on with it…'

'I know you've got a lot of things happening that are causing you trouble. It's affecting your work. How can we help?' Your response is calm and measured. You have moved from Nurturing Parent into Adult. This will block the transaction and the other person will feel that something has changed. The other person's choice then is to stay in Rebellious Child and storm out or move into Adult and discuss the situation.

It is easy to block the transaction. The difficult part is staying in Adult and not getting flicked back to Parent by the other per- son. Often, when a transaction is blocked or crossed, the subject will change and, if the other person changes his or her ego state in response, the previous topic will be forgotten. You will move onto a subject that will move you both forward.

If you try to solve a problem in Parent or Child, you will walk away with the sense that the problem hasn't been solved. You may have addressed some of the symptoms, but your feeling is that the problem is still sitting there, even if things seem better for the moment. When you handle problems from Adult, there is a strong sense that the problem has been solved. This should give you a clue as to which ego state you've been operating from when attempting to handle a problem.

If you try to solve a problem in Parent or Child, you will walk away with the sense that the problem hasn't been solved.

Summary

Leaders are cause, they make things happen. And when people are cause, they feel in control.

- If you are cause, the other person will feel at-the-effect, or in a subordinate role. If the other person is another manager, he or she will not like feeling subordinate to you.
- If you are cause, the person who is at-the-effect may become very defensive, or may strongly resist you, your ideas and your suggestions.
- The most effective way to deal with someone who is cause is to be at-the-effect.
- Parent, Adult and Child ego states can trigger the other person into a complementary ego state and create emotion that gets in the way of the communication.
- The Parent ego state provides and enforces conduct and sets

the standards and limits. If you are in the Parent ego state, you reproduce your parents' behaviour, including their inhibitions, their reasoning, their impulses and their emotions. Your responses are not appropriate to the situation.

- When you are in the Child ego state, you reproduce behaviours, feelings and experiences from your own childhood. Your responses are not appropriate to the situation.

- To take responsibility and change, you need a commitment from the Adult ego state, not a promise from the Child ego state — 'I'll try'.

- When you are in the Adult ego state, you respond to the here-and-now in an appropriate manner as an adult. This leads to problem-solving.

6 THE PUZZLE OF LOW SELF- ESTEEM

Imagine this. Jeremy is a promotions director for your company. He has vast experience in his industry. He manages quite a large department, and is constantly facing demands from clients that he work on their campaigns. Most years, either he or people in his department are recognised nationally by the awards they win. From your point of view, Jeremy is one of the reasons that clients are loyal to your company.

But Jeremy is one of your biggest frustrations. And worse still, not only is he creating frustration within the management team, he is single-handedly breaking down the cooperation that once existed between his and the other departments. In the past, veiled comments were made about Jeremy — sarcasm occasionally leaked out at management meetings — but now you have a stream of managers and staff coming to talk to you about the problems they are having with him. You finally have to admit Jeremy is a problem when his own staff start saying that they're getting pretty frustrated, too.

The real problem is that you can't quite put your finger on the problem. Jeremy has so much going for him. He is creative, he's a really Nice Guy, and, while he's fairly quiet, clients like the concepts he comes up with for them. But he's driving people in the office nuts.

Jeremy seems to hide his head in the sand. If there's a problem in his department, Jeremy has a client meeting to go to. Every time you want to talk to him about some of the problems, Jeremy has a client concept that is right on deadline. And that's one of the problems — Jeremy doesn't seem to want to face or handle the problems.

When you do get him cornered, he gets very defensive about his staff. It is difficult in a management meeting to even discuss some issues because you know that Jeremy is taking it all personally. You and the other managers don't want to hurt him, so, to begin with, you are careful. Then, as the frustration builds, you get impatient. As you get more impatient, you become critical and some of your opinions become accusations. Sound familiar? Take a moment to look at the consequences of this scenario.

As you reach a point where your patience has run out and you are starting to make judgements against him, you'll automatically become more critical of him. Initially, you'll avoid eye contact. This, as you will learn later in this chapter, reinforces his lack of worth in his own eyes. In other words, your body language, which delivers eighty per cent of your communication, will say to him that he is a fake, that he isn't worth a lot as a person. And, yes, he is taking this personally. As you get more frustrated, you'll start to push harder to get problems solved or to get him to cooperate with solving some of the problems between departments. Now you hold eye contact aggressively. This will make Jeremy even more defensive; he will try to avoid both you and the issue. And, yes, he will take everything you say and do personally. Because Jeremy, who has worked his way up to the top of his profession, who is recognised nationally and is paid accordingly, and who manages a highly successful promotions department, has low self-esteem.

Identifying low self-esteem
How do you identify a person who has low self-esteem? Most of us would describe people who are down and out and appear to have no pride in themselves or their lives. Or they would describe someone who is on drugs, or perhaps the battered housewife. You know that one of the reasons these people continue in these circumstances is because they have low self-esteem. This is what the experts say.

But what about low self-esteem in the apparently successful person? In your team? Your managers? Your boss? The people who act a little over the top and appear to be confidence personified, the people who have everything they could want, can also have low self-esteem. How does a successful person have low self-esteem? What does the well-dressed person with a good job and reasonable money have in common with the more obvious examples of low self-esteem? And more importantly, what impact does people's low self-esteem have on those around them?

You're probably reading this book to help you manage your team or your boss better. Well, chances are that some of your people will have low self-esteem. And if your self-esteem is high, you will have almost no understanding of what makes them tick or how they operate. To help, support and move them towards consistent success, you are going to have to open your mind and suspend your belief that black is black and white is white. What I'm going to explain to you is not going to make a lot of sense, initially.

People with low self-esteem may be attractive, even beautiful. They may be successful business owners, or they may be wealthy. But they won't be consistently successful, and what they've done will never be good enough. They will attribute their success to luck. They won't recognise their good attributes at all, or, alternatively, will boast to you about what they've done to get the feedback and recognition they so desperately need. If they don't feel good about themselves, they will be driven to prove to the world how good they are verbally, or with material possessions, or through their partner. They will need to bring their success to your attention and have you recognise their worth. People with low self-esteem don't recognise their own value, so they desperately need recognition from you and every other person they meet. Or they will play down their talent in the fear that if you take too much notice of them, you might discover what they are really like.

> **People with low self-esteem don't recognise their own value, so they desperately need recognition from you and every other person they meet.**

There is a difference between confidence and self-esteem. Self-confidence is believing you can do it, self-esteem is believing that you deserve the good results from doing it.

> **Self-confidence is believing you can do it, self-esteem is believing that you deserve the good results from doing it.**

Let's take a step back and look behind this in order to understand it better. Available data tells us that young women, when they fail, are more likely than men to say 'I am bad' rather than 'What I did was bad'. Therefore, when something bad happens, it is their fault. Have you ever seen an interview with a woman who was stuck in a relationship with a violent man? She will often take the blame for causing the violence. 'It was my fault, I forgot to tape the program he wanted to watch.' So, when her partner explodes in a raging fury, she believes that it is her fault, not that her behaviour only gave him an excuse for his behaviour — it was her.

Most people with low self-esteem are also pessimists. They believe that bad events will last forever. The problems are insurmountable, will undermine everything they do, and most importantly, the problems are their own fault.

People with low self-esteem will wallow in defeat. People with healthy self-esteem will see obstacles as problems that can be solved, they just have to find the right plan. They see problems as surmountable and separate from themselves. Pessimists can't snap out of their pessimism because they believe the problem is permanent, it will be with them for the rest of their life. They have to live with it. Even small obstacles can seem to be giant barriers. This means that they worry more than people with healthy self-esteem and anticipate others' reactions to everything they do. This can immobilise them when it comes to making decisions.

Low self-esteem in the workplace
How does this affect you in a work situation? Let's say you've asked the new sales clerk, Ted, to put together the training manuals you need for

Friday's training meeting. You've stated very clearly what you want him to do. As far as you can see, there shouldn't be any obstacles, but, just in case, you ask, 'Do you understand?' He nods, and away he goes. When it's time to see if the job is done, you find, to your surprise, that it's either not done or it's not done to your satisfaction. And it irritates you that Ted avoids eye contact with you. You assume that this means he knows he's done a lousy job and feels guilty. So you patiently explain once again how he should do the job. And, once again, you ask him, 'Do you understand now?' He nods and away he goes. You feel a warm sense of accomplishment at having the patience to deal with him. You may decide that the problem is his youth, he doesn't listen, or maybe he's not quite as intelligent as you'd like.

Later, when it still isn't done, you become critical of him because you don't understand why he hasn't been able to do the job. He senses this and withdraws further. Now you can get nothing out of him. Your patience is quickly running out. To relieve your frustration, you turn your attention to Lewis, one of your sales reps.

This rep has the potential to be a top performer. He has the product knowledge, the personality and works hard. But he lets his clients walk all over him, he promises more than he can deliver, and more importantly, when things go wrong, he tries to look the other way. And when things do go wrong, it really knocks him off his perch. The other thing that worries you is his appalling relationship with his partner. He talked to you about it, just before he left his partner. The relationship was constant arguments with verbal abuse on both sides. It was really distracting him and pulling his focus off his job.

Unbelievably, he went back to her. You'd think that he liked being in a lousy relationship. But you know how unhappy he is, and it worries you because it's affecting his work on a regular basis. Besides, it makes no sense. If he's so unhappy, why doesn't he leave? And once he's left, why can't he stay away

The healthy self-esteem disadvantage

In both these cases you are suffering from the healthy self-esteem disadvantage. You've attempted to put yourself in their shoes and yet you have no idea about how they see things or why they act the way they do. In the first case, you have imagined yourself doing Ted's job. The steps you would take and what you'd do are quite obvious. If you were doing it, it would be done in no time flat. Your focus is on *your* knowledge, *your* ability to get the job done. You haven't any perception of Ted apart from being a receptacle for your instructions.

The second case doesn't make any sense to you at all. If it was you, you'd be gone from the relationship immediately.

The low self-esteem point of view
People with low self-esteem believe that you can treat them in any way you think they deserve. If you are rude to them, if you walk all over them, that's all they deserve, so why should they object? They've probably done something that they shouldn't have anyway, so it's partly their fault. Their objective is to make you happy because your happiness is much more important than theirs, so if treating them badly makes you happy that's okay with them. Lewis stays in a bad relationship at least partly because he has low self-esteem. He may think he's lucky to have a relationship at all.

If Ted suffers from low self-esteem, it will prevent him from speaking up and saying his workload is too heavy to get the training manuals done, or that he hasn't done this kind of job before and needs training. He may not even be able to ask you questions unless the situation is totally unthreatening for him. He will nod his head and keep his worries to himself. He will take the blame for not being able to do the job. It is not that he has too much of a workload, it's because he is hopeless and not worth keeping on the payroll. It is not that he doesn't understand because no one has ever explained the way this job is meant to be done, it's because he is so stupid. He takes everything personally, blaming himself for not getting the job done.

Ted will go to any lengths to avoid embarrassing or humiliating himself. He'll do this by not contributing or participating in any discussion you try to have with him. Therefore, he can't tell you that he hasn't got time to do your training manuals, he will hide this fact and agree to do them for you. It will be very difficult for him to admit this.

He'll go to any lengths to hide a mess or mistake; protecting himself and saving face will be his driving force. He will agree with anything you say so that you'll go away and leave him alone.

He will prefer to fade into the background. If you suspect he has low self-esteem and compliment him on his work, he simply won't believe that you mean what you say. Acknowledge his contribution to the team, and he'll think you are just being nice. Compliments don't build self-esteem, even if they are genuine.

> **Compliments don't build self-esteem, even if they are genuine.**

People with low self-esteem focus entirely on themselves. This means that their awareness is limited. Their senses are working overtime to ensure they do nothing to upset you or anybody else they come in contact with. They wear blinkers that only allow them to see all the ways in which they might do things wrongly. Low self-esteem makes it difficult for them to see the reality of the situation. They will always blame themselves for anything that goes wrong, regardless of whether it is so or not.

> **People with low self-esteem focus entirely on themselves.**

Lewis can't stand up to his clients because they might think less of him. So he protects himself by agreeing with whatever they ask for and promises extra, although he knows deep down that he probably won't be able to deliver. He's protecting himself, not being honest with himself or his client and, sooner or later, will be faced with having to try to get this past his manager. When you point out to him that what he promised was against company policy, he will agree that he knew that but he thought that just this once you'd make an exception. You'll be wondering if you have seriously misjudged him. And you'll be doubting Ted's ability to do anything but the most basic of jobs. You may be starting to doubt your own ability to hire competent staff.

What destroys self-esteem?

Basically, we have an essential inner nature unique to each of us. If this inner nature is permitted to guide our life, we grow healthy, fruitful and happy. This inner nature is delicate and subtle, and easily overcome by habit, cultural pressure and negative attitudes towards it. Phrases like, 'You're too big for your boots', or 'Who do you think you are?' shrivel self-esteem in both children and adults. Often the suppression of this inner nature is reflected in their environment, their health, their relationships and the type of friends they choose.

If this essential core of people is denied or suppressed, they get sick, sometimes in obvious ways, sometimes in subtle ways, sometimes immediately, sometimes later. This often shows up when people with fragile self-esteem are very successful at something. They will get sick immediately afterwards and be prevented from sustaining the success. Even if something good does happen to them, they don't feel they deserve it, so they do something that doesn't appear to be their fault to diminish the result and allow them to move back into their comfort zone of struggle. While this doesn't make sense logically, and you know they desperately want to change their circumstances, it happens consistently.

Research done recently in America showed that some very subtle things affect self-esteem. They measured the self-esteem of boys and girls starting college, and again when they graduated. They found that, on the whole, boys' self-esteem had strengthened, and they blamed any low grades on the teachers or the school. With the girls, there was a different result. On the whole, their self-esteem had dropped. They blamed themselves severely for not getting good grades, for not being popular or slimmer.

The research continued and identified what experiences were affecting the girls negatively. They found that in the classroom itself, the teacher had far less eye contact with the girls and talked over the top of them more often. So, the boys got more eye contact. When the boys spoke, the teacher not only stopped and listened to them, but heard them out uninterrupted. These two small behaviours sent big subconscious messages to the girls. Eighty per cent of communication is non-verbal, so these behaviours told the girls that they were not as important. As the message sank in, the girls became a little more withdrawn and unsure. The teachers became impatient with trying to draw the girls out, and their consequent reaction reinforced the girls' belief that they were not only not as important, but they were a nuisance and a problem.

Now, not all girls get the same message or react in the same way, but give someone enough subtle messages about their importance and it will change the way they think about themselves. It will impact on their self-esteem.

Managing low self-esteem

There are ways of managing people with low self-esteem, for your benefit and for theirs. Giving Ted, for example, another set of instructions and sending him on his way reinforces his low self-esteem. You are doing his thinking for him. This only reinforces that he is not a capable being; it confirms his low self-esteem. On the other hand, if Ted gets to think for himself and accomplish something, he will start to value himself more. Everything that reinforces the image we have of ourselves keeps the pattern of behaviour in place. Every message that opposes that image helps break the pattern. Everything that reinforces the image we have of ourselves keeps the pattern of behaviour in place.

Every message that opposes that image helps break the pattern.

> **Everything that reinforces the image we have of ourselves keeps the pattern of behaviour in place. Every message that opposes that image helps break the pattern.**

So, guiding Ted through the steps he needs to take to make things happen, giving him responsibility and letting him do it himself, is the key to strengthening his self-esteem. Stretching his comfort zone slowly but surely by giving him jobs that he thinks he can't do and discovers he can, will do more for his self-confidence and happiness than anything else you can do for him.

Don't expect everything to change, though. You will see his self-esteem grow; you will see him walk taller and take pride in his accomplishments. You will feel proud, and rightly so, that you've had a positive effect on his development. But at the first obstacle Ted faces, you'll find that deeply ingrained opinion of himself is still in place, despite the fact that he has proven again and again how capable he is. He will drop back into taking the blame and taking it personally, and may not come and tell you that there is a problem until he has worked himself up to such an extent that it is obvious to you that there is something wrong. If you encourage him to come and talk to you next time and save himself weeks of worry, that invitation will not make it any easier for him to come to you when he has the next problem. He will always try to cope on his own, and will again despair of finding a solution. He will always feel it is his fault, it is his problem and it is up to him to find a solution.

It is this recurring theme that tries most people's patience and causes them to decide that it is just too much hard work trying to help people in this situation. To try your patience even further, they may have recurring health problems. People with healthy self-esteem often have better health and better health habits. This is because they nurture and care about themselves. People with low self-esteem tend to take less care of themselves.

Youth and low self-esteem

When you add the insecurity of youth to behaviour based on low self-esteem, some of the reasons that some young people are unable to hold a job for long become clearer. If young people with low self-esteem work with an insensitive manager or a supervisor who simply doesn't understand why these young people can't do the job, the young person will feel rejected, will resent the boss, and will leave or be sacked. In the business world today, we don't have time to be concerned about such casualties. We just keep burning young people until we find one who works by our standards to our satisfaction.

The tragedy of this is that we usually give young people to our lowest-level supervisors to manage. Often these supervisors have no training in supervising or managing others. They may have poor management practices, such as verbal abuse. And when young people strike back verbally in an inappropriate manner, they get the sack. You may think the way I used to, that once young people have a job it's up to them to work hard and keep it. But I have since sat many times with young people who earnestly ask for strategies on how to deal with abusive and unacceptable behaviour from their bosses so that they could keep their jobs. Managers of young people, even managers of one young person, need solid training in supervising and managing others.

Low self-esteem in managers and bosses

In a management meeting, you complain about the finance manager's assistant. The finance manager, Ilse, takes any criticism about her, her department or staff, personally. Rather than look at the situation and assess it objectively for the truth of the matter, Ilse flies into protection mode and usually attacks the person making the complaint. She may go back and discuss the situation with the relevant staff member, but she will do it by being on her staff member's side and will make the other manager wrong for criticising.

This has become a bit of an issue — it is obvious that Ilse feels rejected when her team is criticised. The rest of the management team become very careful around her. Problems that arise from her department are either avoided or the other departments work around them. In an attempt to help, others may tell Ilse how she should be handling her staff or they may finally become openly critical of her. Both behaviours destroy her self-esteem further by reinforcing the fact that she believes others think she doesn't know how to do her job. In other words, they have discovered that deep down she is useless and doesn't know what she is doing, despite the evidence of years of work to the contrary.

Ilse is also highly vulnerable to the moods and feelings of her staff, peers, clients, boss, partner and anyone else she comes in contact with. The criterion for decision-making for managers with low self-esteem is that no blame should be attached to them, no matter how impractical that decision may be in the long term.

> **The criterion for decision-making for managers with low self-esteem is that no blame should be attached to them, no matter how impractical that decision may be in the long term.**

You have the most chance of success in handling the problem with the person in Ilse's department if you discuss it with Ilse in a quiet, calm environment, instead of raising it in a management meeting. Because she is defensive of her staff, anyone watching or listening will magnify her reaction. You avoid being aggressive, accusing or heavy cause, and keep the tone conversational and low key. If Ilse feels that you are supporting her and her staff, she will be much more open to admitting there is a problem. This approach takes time and patience. But it's your problem.

Investing some time into solving it may be the most productive thing to do.

Some high profile and highly successful people have low self-esteem. They take huge risks that, if they pull them off, make them look fantastic. But if they fail, which most do eventually, they do it in a big way.

Four-star general Norman Schwarzkopf tells what makes a leader in the war room or the living room. 'Ninety-nine per cent of leadership failures have not been failures of competence. They've been failures of character, ethics and integrity.' Character, ethics and integrity can only exist with a strong, healthy self-esteem.

Low self-esteem in clients

If you have clients with low self-esteem, they will be afraid of making wrong decisions. They will want to see lots of evidence that what you are suggesting is going to be the right thing for them to choose. They will want to get from you ways in which they can justify their decisions, such as statistics, a guarantee if things go wrong, or evidence that others have made the same decision and it has worked for them.

They will want lots of support through the decision-making process. This means that if you are a bit of a Nice Guy and back off at the point of leading them to make a decision, you are removing their support right at the time they need it the most. They will need you to be very confident that they are doing the right thing. Any doubt or lack of confidence from you at this point, and they will back off. They will need you to be very patient; to rush them may panic them and increase their fear of making the wrong decision. If they feel you understand them and their business, that you are fully supportive and have given them confidence that they are making the right decision, you will get a decision from them. If they decide against you and you still support them and offer to help if anything at all goes wrong, they will remember and call on you next time they have any doubts. The main thing to remember with clients who have low self-esteem is to offer them your full support. It is tempting to get impatient with them because you don't understand why they can't make a decision.

Summary

If your self-esteem is high, you will have almost no understanding of what makes people with low self-esteem tick or how they operate.

- Don't ask 'Do you understand?', ask 'Do you think there is anything that might stop you from getting this done?'
- Beware of focusing on your knowledge and your ability as if you were going to get the job done.
-

When people have low self-esteem:

- their attention is on themselves
- their whole focus is on protecting themselves, and they will go to any lengths to avoid being embarrassed or humiliated
- they will just want to fade into the background
- they live in a constant state of over-anticipation in the fear of the inevitable, that they are going to make a mistake.
-

If you do the thinking for people with low self-esteem, it reinforces their low self-esteem and lack of self-value further. If people get to think for themselves and accomplish something, they will start to build their self-esteem.

If managers have low self-esteem, their decision-making criteria will revolve around avoiding taking the blame. Any suggestion that their staff are inefficient they will take as personal criticism.

7 DELEGATION

Angelo was the general manager of a large company and had twelve managers reporting to him. He was starting to crumble under the pressure of work, taking home boxes of papers to work on, starting early and working late and, in my opinion, doing some of the work his managers should have been doing themselves. But Angelo claimed all his managers were too busy. He described the extraordinary company growth to me, and the resulting increase in pressure and responsibility on all his managers. Adding to the pressure was that they not only had to manage their departments, but also had clients allocated to them.

Angelo cared about his staff. He could see the pressure they were under and was trying not to make their jobs more difficult by adding to that pressure. But he had a company to run, he had a senior board to answer to and, more importantly, shareholders to please. He had to keep the pressure on, even though it seemed to him that the pressure was increasing on his managers from all sides.

Angelo spoke to me about his problem because he didn't think he could keep the pace up for much longer, and he couldn't see a way out. He was working all the hours he could, and he felt he should be spending more time with his teenage children, not to mention his wife. But any spare time he squeezed out of his week was spent sleeping or sitting like an exhausted zombie.

Firstly, we did an exercise. We imagined he was going to train a new person for his role and we made a list of all the jobs he should be doing. Then we made another list, which was considerably longer and very different, of the things that he actually did each day. And then we compared the two. It came as no surprise to Angelo that he was doing lots of things that he shouldn't. He knew he was doing things that he thought his managers didn't have time to do.

So I asked him, 'How do you know they don't have time to do it?'

'Well, you just have to watch them. They're racing round and they can't even get through what they're meant to be doing, let alone take on this extra work I need them to do.'

'So, how do you know that they're really too busy?' He looked puzzled at such an obviously stupid question. 'They tell me! I ask them to do something for me and they get in a panic and tell me about the client project they've got to finish, or the accounts they have to get out on time.'

'And what do you do when they tell you that?'

'Well, I don't want to hold up a client's job, so I see if I can get someone else to do it. Or I do it myself, if I can.'

'So telling you all the jobs they have to do is a very successful action.'

He thought about that for a moment, and then saw what I was getting at. He grinned, 'Yes, but they really are very busy. They're not just trying to avoid what I'm asking them to do.' He thought about it for a moment. 'At least, I don't think they are.'

I decided it was time to take the next step in the exercise. 'So, what do you think would happen if you gave them extra jobs to do? Let's take Antoniette for example. You have some items on your list that she should be doing. What do you think would happen if you gave them to Antoniette to do?' I knew that there were many tasks he needed for Antoniette to start doing. She had merged two departments into one. Angelo wasn't getting the information he needed from this new department.

'She'd have to work later than she normally would, and she's usually not out of here before seven every night. It's not fair to her and her family, and I don't want to burn her out.'

'That's fair enough. But let's look at Antoniette's department and see what would happen if she got extra work to do. What could she delegate to her staff?'

Angelo snorted with derision. 'That's one of the problems. Antoniette's got this fellow Joe in her department who is a nine-to-fiver. He leaves on the dot of five every night and, although Antoniette doesn't agree with this, I don't think he pulls his weight. She's got a woman, Evette, who is brilliant, but she answers to Joe, and I believe he's holding her back.'

I recapped the situation. 'So what you're saying is that you can't delegate the work that Antoniette should be doing because Joe is not supportive of her, so she can't in turn delegate to him. In fact, because he is not supportive of her, he increases her workload and is a barrier to another staff member who is supportive. Is that what you're saying?'

I could see Angelo's temper start to rise and thought I'd give it an extra push. 'In fact, what you're really saying is that you are protecting Antoniette because she is protecting Joe who is not supportive of your business. So, what you're all doing is supporting Joe. And whatever he is doing to prevent taking on extra work is a very successful action.'

Now he was really going red in the face. He didn't like that idea at all. He was happy to support his managers, who rewarded him with loyalty and hard work, but there was no way he would support anyone who didn't pull his weight.

'So how do we handle this? We can't just walk in there and sack him. Antoniette wouldn't do that anyway.'

I encouraged him to think it through. 'What would happen if you put more demands on Antoniette? Nothing over the top, just the things that you feel she really should be doing as manager of her department. What do you think would happen?'

'Well, she'd have to delegate some of her existing work to Joe, and, immediately, there'd be a problem.'

'And whose problem would it be?'

'What do you mean?'

'Well, who would have to face the fact that there is a problem and take action about solving it?'

The light went on. 'Antoniette would. It would be Antoniette's problem. She would have to face the fact that she's got a problem in her department.'

'And she would have to do something about it because you're not going to drop the pressure, you're going to increase it,' I finished for him. 'When you delegate, your role is exposed. If you are protecting someone, you are hiding the problem.'

> **If you are protecting someone, you are hiding the problem.**

So, Angelo delegated his work to Antoniette, much to her initial alarm. But Angelo coached her through it, and said that if she had any problems getting the work done she was to come back and talk to him.

When I next saw Angelo, I asked him what had happened. He said that Antoniette had come back to talk to him and Angelo had thought that the whole thing was going to drop back in his lap. But Antoniette had come to talk about Joe. When the pressure went on, Antoniette had looked to Joe for support and had not got it. After talking with Angelo, Antoniette continued to keep the pressure on Joe. He resisted until he handed in his resignation. Now Evette came into her own and Antoniette found her workload reduced as Evette took on even more. Antoniette hired a junior to assist Evette, and is now able to take on even more responsibility.

Angelo said, 'In fact, it worked so well, I delegated work to the other managers, as well.'

'What happened?' After Angelo's earlier description of their workload and the pressure they were already under, I pictured a mutiny or something else almost as dramatic.

'Nothing.' He shook his head in wonder. 'I gave them extra work to do and a deadline. I hardened myself and let them know that no excuses would be acceptable. It had to be done and they knew it. And, without exception, they did it, and did it within time.'

I smiled and wondered if he realised the valuable lesson he had learnt. 'And what does that tell you?'

Angelo sat back in his chair in disbelief. 'All this time, I have been protecting them, worrying about them, trying to do the best for them. They convinced me that they were working to capacity. And it simply wasn't true.' I could see that he felt somewhat betrayed.

'Remember, Angelo, they were just doing what you were doing.

'What was that?'

'They were protecting their staff by not delegating. By putting more pressure on your managers, you forced them to delegate. When you forced them to delegate, you forced them to identify the problems and handle them.'

He'd caught on now, and he added, 'And I have to watch for those successful actions that I so easily buy into.'

'So, what will you say now if your managers tell you that they have client projects they have to get finished and you've asked them to complete something for you?'

He thought for a minute. 'I'll ask them how they're going to get through them both. What can they delegate? Who will they delegate it to? What problems do they think they might encounter in delegating the work? In fact, I'll become their manager, and by forcing them to delegate their work I'll force them to manage their areas as well.'

Why we don't delegate

What gets in the way of successful delegation? Your attitude.

I'm too busy to spend time teaching others how to do things.

They don't do it the way I ask them to do it.

Why would I spend time teaching someone else to do the things I enjoy doing myself?

When I ask people to do it for me, I spend so much time worrying about the job and checking that they're doing it correctly, I might as well do it myself and have peace of mind into the bargain.

I don't have the resources to delegate work.

My problem isn't delegating or the lack of it, mine is that I just don't have enough hours in the day.

I've heard all the rationalisations about not delegating. Rationalisations help us feel better about not doing what we know we should be doing. After all, how important is it that you delegate? It's your job and if you have to work longer hours to get something done properly, it's nobody's problem but yours. Right? Wrong! Think again.

The potential for growth within an organisation is determined by the ability of the managers to delegate. The true roles of a manager are to think, to plan and to train. This is where the potential for growth in an organisation comes from. But these roles take time and concentration, and they are hidden beneath a daily workload that never diminishes. It's almost impossible to concentrate if you are overwhelmed with your workload. And so most managers spend minimal time, if any, on the kind of work that has the most impact on the success of their department and, ultimately, the company. If you are not delegating effectively, you may be restricting the growth of the company. That's a heavy realisation, but it's true.

> **The potential for growth within an organisation is determined by the ability of the managers to delegate.**

Successful delegation occurs more often by accident rather than design. To delegate successfully, there are certain steps to be followed. And if you jump this chapter to get on to something more interesting, you're probably the person who needs to read it the most. Keep reading!

Giving instructions

Often, when delegating, we only tell people what the task is that they have to do. They have no picture of how important the task is, no understanding of the consequences of not doing it to the standard you want or within the time you set.

You want someone to prepare your proposal for you in time for a board meeting the next day. You say, 'Carmen, could you key this proposal for me?' A simple enough instruction, surely. But just to make sure, you say, 'It's very, very important.'

She smiles and assures you that she'll get it done for you, no problems. You walk away with an uneasy feeling that she's not going to

102

get it done, but what more can you say? Surely she understands how important it is.

Late the next morning, everything seems to be going wrong. You had intended to be absolutely organised so that you could be calm for the board meeting. The directors have rattled you a little during the last couple of meetings, and this proposal is important to you and your staff. You know how much it will increase the efficiency of the department if they accept it. But it would seem that it's your day for problems. You grab your briefcase and search your desk for the proposal. Desperately, you call for help. 'Carmen, where's that proposal I asked you to key? Why isn't it sitting on my desk?' You're hoping that her answer is that she has put it in your briefcase, but deep down you just know what the answer is going to be.

'I haven't quite finished it yet. Are you in a hurry for it?'

'Yes! I need it now! I told you it was important!'

You find yourself thinking that you just can't trust anyone to do anything important. And the less you trust people, the less you will delegate.

It is painfully obvious what was missing in this scenario. Firstly, there was no deadline given, and secondly, what does important mean? It's important to you, but what does that mean to Carmen? To delegate successfully, you must make getting the job done as important to your staff as it is to you. If Carmen understands, for example, that the consequence of getting that proposal done in time is that she might get the software she needs to get the computers in the office networking, something she's been waiting impatiently for, she'll put her heart and soul into getting it done. And she'll probably spend extra time making sure that it looks very professional. She'll do whatever it takes to ensure that it gets finished on time. Because now it is important to her as well, and she understands the consequences.

> **To delegate successfully, you must make getting the job done as important to your staff as it is to you.**

Do they understand?

Often when we give instructions we ask, 'Do you understand?' and usually the answer is yes. But what do they understand? When you ask them if they understand, aren't you really asking whether there is anything they can think of that might stop them getting the job done? It might be better to ask them this outright.

> **When you ask them if they understand, aren't you really asking whether there is anything they can think of that might stop them getting the job done?**

Carmen, for example, might then tell you that one of the other managers wants her to put a proposal together for a client presentation first thing tomorrow morning and she has to work on that first. Or, she may tell you that she has a dentist appointment at the end of the day and she needs to know how long the proposal is so she can estimate whether she has enough time to get it done. If she has any doubts, she can bring some help in to handle some of her other jobs.

Also, if Carmen is not confident or has low self-esteem, she won't want to admit that she doesn't think she can get through the workload. So she'll tell you, yes she can get it done, but she won't know how she's going to make this happen. If you ask her what might stop her from getting it done, in a subtle way you are taking the focus off her and putting it onto other external problems. This will be easier for her to handle, and she'll be more open and communicative.

Peace of mind

If you have delegated a job and you find you still have your attention on it, you haven't delegated it correctly. If you have delegated efficiently, it should not need your attention. So, the next step will be for you to set up a system that gives you the feedback you need to reassure you that the job is proceeding according to schedule and to the level of excellence you require.

A vital part of delegation is to decide what kind of feedback you need, and how often you need it. If the job is a big one and very important, you may want regular meetings to discuss progress. You can then redirect your staff if you think it is getting off the track. In Carmen's case, maybe you needed to have a look at a draft of the proposal by the end of the first day.

> **A vital part of delegation is to decide what kind of feedback you need, and how often you need it.**

What you don't do is give your people a job to do and then go and check on them all the time. If it's a keying job you've given them, don't go and stand over them, reading the screens over their shoulders. This is probably one of the most irritating and distracting things you can do. Just ask your support people; they'll tell you, much more forcibly than I can, how annoying it is.

What you do is tell your people what feedback you want, and leave it to them to come to you. This will give them a sense of being in control and will strengthen their sense of responsibility for the job. You can make changes or improvements, and you'll know how things have progressed and how they are going. But they must come to you, you must not hover or keep checking on them. If you are worried about the job being done properly, ask yourself what you have missed in the delegation process. Why don't you trust them to do the job properly for you? Do they need more training?

Roles and responsibility

Effective delegation means your staff take responsibility for getting the job done to your standards and timetable. This means they must become decision-makers. They must ask themselves some questions. Can I cope with the workload and if not, what can I do about it? Who can I go to, to ask for help? What do I have to do to make this happen? If they make no decisions and hope the problems will just go away or miraculously sort themselves out, they haven't taken responsibility for the job.

> **Effective delegation means your staff take responsibility for getting the job done to your standards and timetable. This means they must become decision-makers.**

You may have discouraged your people from becoming decision-makers. After all, you have told them what you want, how you want it and when. You have left no room for decisions, just for them to do as they're told.

I worked with a client who was a partner in an accounting firm. She had three capable young accountants working for her, and a very efficient assistant. But she was the bottleneck for the company. The practice was small, and she and her partner had built strong relationships with their clients. They knew how important it was for their clients to be able to trust them to do things correctly. My client's job was to check everything before it went out. Her desk was surrounded by piles of files, and, even when she left work to go home, she always felt under pressure. She would work long hours and most of her weekends. The thought of taking a holiday horrified her. Things were taking longer and longer, and deadlines were being missed. But what could my client do? She was working as hard as she could.

My feedback to her was that she was working as hard as she could, but her staff were vastly underused. Did she have to check everything? The answer was a resounding yes. Could a level of checking proceed before it came to her?

She thought about it for a moment, and brightened up. 'Do you know, if we got the junior people to check each other's work before it came to me, it would be quite a good learning experience for them.

Especially if they check it and I still find something incorrect, then they will learn what they are overlooking. Not only will it help me, they will be learning through the process.'

The next step was to look at the role of her assistant. She sat with him, explained the situation, and asked him what he thought he could help more with. His answer nearly had her fall out of her chair. He told her that he had thought for some time that there were some forms that he could handle if she would help him learn them. She had assumed only a qualified accountant could follow this process, but she was willing to teach him if he wanted to give it a shot. He amazed her by picking it up quickly and handling it well.

My client thought she was doing exceptionally well. She was now delegating many things that came across her desk. I thought she was doing exceptionally well when she began to delegate things before they got to her doorway.

Now that she was delegating effectively, her true role started to emerge. Effective delegation reveals the true role of the manager. She had been doing work that did not fit into her role because she felt other people were too busy or unable to do it. When she delegated, she found that her staff welcomed the opportunity to take on more responsibility and prove themselves. She was actually allowing them the opportunity to grow and improve.

Effective delegation reveals the true role of the manager.

My client found she now had time to plan, to address the marketing of the company and to put strategies in place that would increase its client base and make it even more successful. This would then make everyone even busier, and so the process would go on. She now goes home before dark, is more cheerful and less stressed. She feels good about her work, and her family appreciates the difference. In fact, she said that she feels as if she's on holiday even when she's working because that pressure is no longer there. She's still busy, but she's doing what is required of her in her role. And her staff are becoming more capable and willingly taking more responsibility than they were before. The foundation is now in place for the company to grow and become more successful.

Attached versus committed

There is another reason why some managers don't delegate. Working towards a goal can lead you to become either attached to the goal or committed to the goal. When you are attached to a goal, it must happen your way. The goal is important, but so is the way the goal is reached. It must be done the way you say. This is an authoritarian management style. The authoritarian style of management takes responsibility away from the people you manage. They are not allowed to choose how to do something.

> **The authoritarian style of management takes responsibility away from the people you manage.**

When you are attached to the goal, you will find lots of evidence to prove doing it your way is right. You will use justifications and rationalisations and there may be lots of emotion, which means you will exert a great deal of pressure. In this situation, the stronger the emotion around getting to the goal, the stronger your reaction will be to anything that is a barrier to achieving the goal. So, if a report isn't done in time your reaction will be extreme. If it doesn't get done your way, you'll spit the dummy because you are right and you want it done your way. The person doing the job has no decisions to make. This style of management does not lend itself easily to delegation.

When you are committed to a goal, you give up the need to be right and give your people room to choose. This is a participative management style. You focus on the result, and leave the details to others. While you are willing to be responsible for doing whatever it takes to get to the goal, you are comfortable with the idea that it could equally well be done your way or someone else's way. You simply explain how the goal is important; you don't tell them how it should happen. The participative style of management motivates the people in your team to take responsibility for making the goal happen. Being committed to a goal can be described as leadership.

> **The participative style of management motivates the people in your team to take responsibility for making the goal happen.**

The most successful leaders use both styles of management. Sometimes, the authoritarian style is appropriate. Good leaders are consciously aware of what they are doing and the results they are creating by the system of management they use.

The final step in delegation

You have delegated the work and you have given a timetable for progress reports. There is one last step you may have to go through. How do you know that they can perform the task the way you want them to? Sure, you can ask them, and they'll tell you that they understand and they know what to do and why. But how do you know?

The first step is to tell your support people exactly what you want them to do. Secondly, you'll probably show them how to do it. You'll get them to watch while you do it. Then you need to get them to teach you how to do it. When you come to teach someone else how to do something, you discover very quickly what exactly isn't clear or what you don't know. This last step, either in delegating or training, is very often overlooked. I cover this more fully in the chapter on motivation.

Summary

When delegating:

- Explain what you need to have done.
- Give a deadline.
- Explain how the task fits into the bigger picture.
- Explain the consequences of it not being done in time or to the standards you require.
- Ask if there's anything that might stop them from getting it done as you have asked.
- Set times for regular reports and feedback on progress.
- Check on your management style. Are you attached to the goal or committed to it? Is it the appropriate style for this situation?

To be sure that your support people can do the delegated task:

- Tell them how to do it.
- Show them how to do it.
- Get them to teach you how to do it.

8 MOTIVATION

Several years ago, I found myself in a situation that would delight any advertising manager. We were one of the last daily evening papers in the country and our competition was an incredibly strong and successful daily morning paper. Everyone read our paper, but advertised in the other. We were looked on as being a very poor second in the marketplace. While we worked hard to look after our advertisers, the competition were often so full that they turned away advertising because they simply could not take any further ads.

The advertisers complained that the paper was so successful that its attitude towards advertisers was too casual. There was no effort to please. Real estate advertisers had wanted to walk en masse from the paper but had not been able to get agreement among all their members. They were frightened of losing momentum in their advertising, and therefore losing business.

From the advertisers' point of view, there was no customer service, no one was listening to anything they had to say. They either had to do things the way the paper wanted, or — tough! The car dealers decided to do something about it. They decided as an industry to blacklist the paper, and they came to us.

I came back from holidays and found I had a new job. I was told to take my pick of the best advertising reps at the paper and, not only look after the car dealers but keep them. So we set out on a journey to discover what we could do for them that they hadn't been getting at the other paper. Their demands were quite reasonable. They wanted better quality photographs so that the cars would be clearer. We changed the type of photographer we had been using, upgraded the equipment and put in a new system that was more flexible to their needs. And we listened to them. We negotiated some issues with them, but most importantly, we listened. Ultimately, some of the dealers trickled back to the other paper, but because we were offering such a good service, we kept an increase of car dealer advertising of forty-six per cent.

Now, while these car dealers had a powerful motivation to create change, this also demonstrates an example of what must happen in successful relationships. There must be exchange in any relationship for it to work. Whether it is a business relationship or a personal relationship, if there is no exchange, the relation- ship will founder. The car dealers were giving their money and their advertising to our competition and felt they were getting nothing in return. If we had given them just the service without the advertisements working, then that exchange wouldn't have worked for long either.

> **There must be exchange in any rela-tionship for it to work.**

This holds for managers and their staff, as well. If you are training, supervising and supporting the people in your team, they should be supporting you by getting results for you. If they are not getting results, there is no exchange in the relationship and the relationship is not going to work. This is easy for managers to overlook.

> **If you are training, supervising and supporting the people in your team, they should be supporting you by getting results for you.**

We recognise this in personal relationships quickly. If you have people constantly borrowing things or constantly needing you to listen to their problems but not all that interested in listening to yours, you quickly tire of the situation and do something about it. But, as managers, we are supposed to support our staff to the best of our ability. And the people in our team should support us in return, with loyalty, attitude, hard work and, more importantly, results. It is very disappointing when we realise that the support and effort is all going one way.

More coaching and more training will not change the situation. What you must do is constantly demand that the people in your team perform. Make them realise that support has to be both ways, that there must be an exchange for the relationship to work. One of several things will happen.

The best possible outcome is that they improve their performance. It may surprise you how often I have seen people improve just because their manager reaches the limit of his or her patience and demands results. The next best possible outcome is that they admit that they don't really know how to do things better. You then have a training issue on your hands, but at least you know what the problem is. The third possible outcome is that they object to the pressure of the demand. Keep the pressure on. If they are in the wrong job, they will resign. If they are a problem person, they will go looking for a more understanding manager.

If your staff lift their performance, your next concern to en- able them to achieve ongoing success is for you to get them to motivate themselves.

What is motivation?
What is your reason for reading this book? You want your people to be successful and you want to be a better manager. Your staff's success will be your success. If you are having little or no impact on them, they are likely to be erratic in their results. Some months they'll exceed their wildest expectations — other months they'll not even make budget. And they'll have little or no understanding of what they're doing that makes the difference. They'll point a finger at the economy, their clients, what it's like 'out there', but seldom look at what *they* are doing that contributes towards these results. They may identify that they haven't

been doing enough cold calling, get themselves back on track and eventually hit budget again, but the whole process will be very much hit-and-miss.

Your role is to help them become more capable and consistently more successful. What do you have to do to make this happen? Firstly, you need to be able to identify what they are doing that is stopping this from happening. Secondly, you need to get them to take responsibility for the results they are getting. Remove the blame of outside influences. If the problem is the economy or the time of the year, they can't solve it. There is nothing they can do about their results. You have a problem, but the reps don't. After all, they can't change the economy, can they? Get the people in your team to identify what *they* are doing that contributes to their results. Get them to take responsibility for their results. Work with them to identify what they are good at and what they are weak at. Look at the good months they have had, and ask them to identify what they were doing that worked well for them. Look at their bad months, and identify what they were doing differently. Don't fall into the trap of telling them what they're not doing well. You have to get them to tell you!

> **Get the people in your team to identify what *they* are doing that contributes to their results. Get them to take responsibility for their results.**

Thirdly, you need to create the desire in them to want to change these results. Motivation: the buzz word in sales from the year dot. How often do you hear a comment about a course or training that goes like this: 'We came out of the course really buzzing, it was great! But by a week later it was gone, and we never really did anything different.'

Clearly, true motivation did not occur. Motivation is the process that arouses, *sustains* and regulates human behaviour. Motivation leads to a change in human behaviour because the motivation is sustained until the behaviour is changed. Inspiration, on the other hand, is an arousal of mind and feelings that may or may not (more often not) be strong enough to create a change in behaviour. While we can be inspired by others' words or actions, very often it is not strong enough to induce us to change the way we behave.

> **Motivation is the process that arouses, *sustains* and regulates human behaviour.**

We have good reasons for behaving the way we do, so we need an even better reason to change. And inspiration often doesn't give us a better reason. It stirs our emotions and gives us a glimpse of how we'd like to be, a glimpse of what we're capable of being.

> **We have good reasons for behaving the way we do, so we need an even better reason to change.**

Few people understand how motivation works. Very often the success of a company is the direct result of the natural or learned ability of the chief executive officer to motivate his or her staff to achieve extraordinary results. When this leader moves on, there is a turnover of staff and a drop in performance. Motivation creates intense loyalty to both the leader and, through that person, the organisation. When that leader leaves, the new leader is often found to be lacking in comparison to the previous one and the culture of the place changes, hence the turnover of staff.

Motivating people

There is no one way of motivating people. It takes a combination of conscious and planned approaches. Some of the best motivators I know consciously plan and implement actions designed for the results they achieve. It's not just a lucky talent they were born with, but a deliberate and non-spontaneous approach to caring for and motivating their people.

The first step is to identify what your staff value. Go through the process of identifying the real value, and give your people more of what they value. This has two effects. The first is that they will feel as if the company values them just by being involved in the process, and the second is that you find out what they value so you can give them more of it. If they get what they value, they will be motivated.

> **The first step is to identify what your staff value.**

The second step is to identify where your staff need help and training. Easy, you might think, but this is a much bigger task. This means that you need to be monitoring how well your people are doing and not accepting their excuses for things not going as well as they should be. You may discover that they're in the wrong job. Or that they need training on specific skills.

> **The second step is to identify where your staff need help and training.**

For example, good salespeople may not have good organisational skills. This means that they won't plan well, they'll neglect their paperwork, lose files and lose important pieces of paper. They'll race out the door unprepared for a meeting they had for- gotten about. Chasing around trying to fix things will take up a lot of their time. All these extra activities eat into the time that an efficient salesperson would spend in front of clients or searching out new clients.

You might coach these people yourself. You'll make them aware of how much time they presently waste, getting them to see the reality of what they do (a walk through hell). Then get them to see how their life would be different if they were organised (a walk through heaven). You'll design systems with them to help them become more organised; you'll spend time and effort checking that they are sticking to the systems. You will form an agreement with them to identify what they want and what they are prepared to do to achieve it. Get them to agree to follow agreed systems and give you the authority to police them. You will become their conscience until their new behaviour becomes a new habit.

The unconscious incompetent

People pass through four levels of competency. The first level is the unconscious incompetent — they don't know what they don't know; there's no pain. They can't improve because they don't know what they are doing wrong. If they are successful, it's by default rather than by deliberate strategies. Therefore, their performance is going to be slow and erratic, to say the least.

It's like the weekend golfer who goes out each weekend and happily whacks the ball around, content to have played a game of golf. Then he starts to compare himself to other golfers he sees on the greens. He watches their putting, he gulps at their magnificent drives down the fairway, and becomes dissatisfied with his own performance. At this stage, he doesn't know precisely what he is doing wrong: he's an unconscious incompetent.

To move from the level of the unconscious incompetent, your people must first realise, believe and agree that there is room for improvement. And as their manager and trainer, you have to take them through a three step process:

- Show them how to do it.
- Watch them do it.
- Have them teach you how to do it.

When you show them how to do it, you need to give them specific instructions. Focus on what you want them to do and how you want them to do it. Take them back to basics, step by step, while you supervise closely. At this stage, they are not in a position to question your methods or systems, or try to improve them. This is how learners distract trainers so they don't have to do the basics. They had a better way of doing it at the last place they worked. At this stage, tell them that this is the way we do it here and when they are at level 3, they will have earned the right to improve an already successful method. In fact, not only do they not know how to do it, they don't know which questions to ask, even though they might think otherwise.

The next step is to watch them do it. You might be tempted to leave them to do what has been asked for and, if they get a result, assume that they are effective at the job. Unless you have watched them do what you wanted, to your satisfaction, three times without your supervision, don't assume that they have the skills. You might want to let them off the hook, thinking that they will pick it up sooner or later, but they will be picking up bad habits that will be difficult to change. Also, if you don't watch them, you won't know which skills they haven't yet learnt.

Most managers miss the last vital step: having them teach you how to do it. If you want to find out what you don't know about a subject, try teaching it to others. Having the people you are training teach you how to do it will show both you and them very clearly what they still don't understand. It will create discussion about why certain steps are important and probably bring to the surface many things you take completely for granted. These things can then also be taught. When you have been through this process, the people you are training move to the next level.

The conscious incompetent

Now they know exactly what they are doing wrong — they are conscious incompetents. The golfer becomes aware of the problems with his swing, his putting, his stance, and he makes a decision. He becomes motivated to improve! In fact, at this stage, he may get carried away and decide he wants to be the best. He'll rush out and buy all the books and videos on golf. He may trade his clubs in for a better set in a brand name bag, and search for a golf professional to teach him. He's about to move to the next stage. Be aware, though, that some people don't leave this level. They never get past talking about the improvements they're going to make, the book they're going to write, the systems they're going to implement at work.

This level requires specific tasks be set with close supervision to satisfactory completion. Until the people you are training have achieved the tasks to your satisfaction at least three times without your supervision, you cannot assume that they have gained the skills they need.

The conscious competent

Our weekend golfer is now taking lessons that are pushing out the boundaries of his comfort zone. He feels awkward, embarrassed, stupid. Imagination and emotion are more powerful than thoughts or logic. This is the level where he is most likely to go back to his old way of doing things. He needs to work at doing things the right way consistently, regardless of how they make him feel. His emotions, his self-esteem and his ego will be challenged at this level. He may come up with excuses and rationalisations: 'I only wanted to be a weekend golfer, anyway. It's not as if I wanted to win tournaments or anything.' This is where you learn how strong his motivation is.

> **Imagination and emotion are more powerful than thoughts or logic.**

This level takes effort and determination to continue, no matter what it takes. If the results don't seem worth the effort, the discomfort and the frustration, the people you are training will drop back to the old ways of doing things. This is where a coach is needed, to remind them of what they are aiming for, to keep their goals clear in their minds and to keep them focused. Focus will diminish the emotion, the awkwardness and the insecurity they now feel about their abilities.

You can now take the skills to a higher level of efficiency. Now that they are able to do what is required, you can put more pressure on, such as giving a time frame. For salespeople who have been learning cold calling, you may set a target of five appointments a week from the cold calls. You are moving them from effectiveness to becoming more efficient.

At this level, your people are capable of self-criticism. They will know what they have done wrong or left out, and will be able to address it, or at least ask for help on the specific skill. Actions that originally seemed awkward and made them feel self-conscious, will have become normal and natural.

A trap for managers is to assume that their people are at this level. You assume that they can grow through their own self- criticism because you can. You are happy to be there for them to help and support them, but you expect them to ask for help if they need it. But what if they're not at this level and don't know what questions to ask? Do you know that your people are at this level, or are you making the mistake of assuming their competence?

The unconscious competent

Now many of our golfer's swings are automatic — he doesn't have to think about them anymore. His stance and his grip on the club are now comfortable and his focus is completely on the result he is trying to achieve rather than on himself. He's now achieving good scores consistently, or as consistently as you can in golf! He may decide to start the whole process over again on one particular skill and take himself willingly to another level of excellence.

Of course, people can be at different levels on different jobs at the same time. Sales reps, for example, may be unconscious incompetents in cold calling and unconscious competents in face-to-face meetings with clients.

Once they have reached this level of unconscious competence, they have earned the right to improve on what you have taught them. You should now encourage them to pull apart methods and systems to innovate, modify and maintain them.

Deciding what to train

List the people in your company who come in contact with your customers. This might include salespeople, the receptionist, creative people or technical people.

Now rate how much training they receive:

- for a high level of ongoing training (which is what sales people seem to receive exclusively within many companies)
- for the occasional course once they identify a problem they're having (this is often how supervisory training is instigated)
- for training on their duties when they started the job.

Now rate how much company information they receive:

- for ongoing and updated information
- for receiving information on the company when they started the job

- if you're not even sure how much information they got when they started, apart from where the toilets and lunch room were.

This will give you a place to start from to assess the training needs and information flow in your company.

Think about offering more than duties-only training. What would happen in your company if your technical people were trained in relationship-building and communication skills? One company I know gave its service staff training in communication skills and their service contracts were extended from twelve months to three years. These technical people are now actively building relationships in their largest client company, and are feeding these names back into their company's newsletter database.

> **Think about offering more than duties-only training.**

Training is so much more than just sending your people off for the day to update their computer skills or sales skills. As their manager, it is your job to help them become more capable. You can only do this if you are aware of how they could do their job better and the range of skills they need to achieve what you expect of them.

The skills you need for this are observation and objectivity. You need the energy and time for this. And lastly, but most importantly, you need to care about them enough to give it a try.

One very successful owner of a chain of hairdressing salons has the best training program I've seen anywhere. Every month a ghost customer is given $100 to go to one of her salons and have his hair done. He then fills out a questionnaire. As all the staff know there's a ghost customer every month, every client they get could be that ghost customer, so their performance is kept to a high level.

Apart from the obvious questions about whether the client was happy with his hair, a range of questions are asked that indicate which kind of training (other than hairdressing expertise) the hairdressers need.

- Did the hairdresser recommend shampoo, conditioner or any other products? This is an indicator of sales skills.
- Did you feel the hairdresser was listening to you? This recognises the emotional needs of the client. People like to chat with their hairdressers.
- How much money do you have left from $100? This indicates whether the sales skills were successful or not.

Training managers

Many managers assess their staff training adequately, but completely miss the point of their own role when they come to assessing their own training needs. They search for ways in which they can become more efficient, and this usually involves some form of computer training. Or they try to find ways in which they can learn more about the industry they're in by gaining industry- based knowledge. The one area they tend not to think carefully about is their people handling skills. Because efficiency, knowledge and the impact on the bottom line are always in the spotlight, that's what they focus on. But another certificate on the wall counts for nothing if your staff turnover is high.

Eighty per cent of problems within a manager's job need good people handling skills. Most managers are promoted into management because of their technical or product knowledge, or sometimes simply because of their seniority. Once they become managers, they need good people handling skills. And as Philippe Denichaud, a Canadian management consultant, says, 'We assume that our managers have good people handling skills because they are a people!'

> **'We assume that our managers have good people-handling skills because they are a people!'**

In my experience, managers with poor people handling skills are one of the biggest causes of unmotivated staff. Managers like this create an environment of misunderstanding and frustration that will undermine any exchange that may be in place. Training in people handling skills should be a major priority. An even bigger concern is that most managers don't assess themselves in this area, and neither does their senior management.

Managers with good technical skills are often task oriented. This means that they will overlook the needs of the people involved. If there is a problem, they will spend more time examining the systems and the processes than identifying what emotional and people oriented issues might be relevant. Often this is quite simply because they don't know how to handle them. They would rather handle logical things than emotional beings. Logic is easy to handle; emotion is a minefield. If you want to be a good manager, it will be one of the most difficult jobs to attempt.

Feedback on your people handling skills should be within your appraisal system, where your staff assesses your management. If there is no section in your appraisal forms for your people to assess your management skills from their point of view, it's likely that there is no exchange for them in other areas also. Think about it.

Summary
Motivation is the process that arouses, *sustains* and regulates human behaviour. To motivate your people:
- identify what they value and give them more of it
- identify where they need help and training and provide it.

Training is part of motivating.

People move through four levels as they learn new skills and need appropriate support at each level:
- unconscious incompetent
- conscious incompetent
- conscious competent
- unconscious competent.

Assess the levels of training of the people within your department.
- Are they getting duties-only training and do they need more?
- Do they need some help with some specific skills?
- Are you assuming competence in any of your people?
- Are you assuming competence in any of your own skills?

Managers need training in good people handling skills.
Poor people handling skills are one of the biggest causes of unmotivated staff.

Eighty per cent of problems within a manager's job need good people handling skills.

9 THE FORMULA FOR PEAK PERFORMANCE

If you have ever watched one of your people soar like an eagle one month and then drop like a shot duck the next month, this chapter is for you.

Top performers — we envy them and make limited attempts to copy them, but deep down we believe that, somehow, they were just born that way. Smarter, luckier and harder working than we are able to be. They have a smarter family, fewer worries, better clothes sense, smarter friends, the list is endless. This lets us off the hook of studying them closely so that we can become top performers, too.

Top performers are inspiring to be around, but to learn from them we need to identify the subtle things they do. We need to study them, to watch what they do and how they do it. If you do this, it will soon become obvious that they excel in the management of their systems and in their personal performance. Whatever they do, they are totally absorbed by the task at hand. Their success appears to be effortless because they make it look easy. They are creative and energetic, and, what's more, they usually seem to be enjoying themselves.

Their awareness is high, and this means that they notice even small details. Even though they follow some basic systems, they are spontaneous and take their gut feeling very seriously. They have a certainty, a knowing, which makes you want to unravel their minds to find the secret of their success.

When you experience this state yourself, you are blissfully absorbed. You may be incredibly busy, but you feel relaxed and highly focused rather than stressed. Tasks that were once frustratingly mundane become satisfying in themselves and therefore don't get postponed. Anxiety is replaced by certainty.

There is no focus on self, which means no focus on the preoccupation and small worries of daily life. You respond easily to changing conditions, demands and obstacles. And, amazingly, you become almost unconcerned with how you are doing; you have no thoughts of failure. The sheer pleasure of performing the task at hand is what motivates you.

Most salespeople get glimpses of what it's like to perform at this peak level — a day or a week in which they felt they were 'in flow', when everything they touched worked, everything they had been working on brought in results. They get a tantalising taste of what it would be like to perform at their peak and stretch beyond their existing limits. It's a heady experience, and one that most salespeople are unable to sustain.

There is a formula for staying in flow. The state of being in flow is attainable for anyone willing to work the formula. But working the formula brings success and, strangely, people then have to deal with the fear they have of success. When people first experience being in flow by consciously applying the formula, they drop back again quite quickly afterwards. It's heady stuff up there and frighteningly easy.

Don't underestimate the challenge this poses to our belief in ourselves, our friends, our families and our careers. People around us, family and friends, can react quite strongly when we first start moving towards success. While on the surface they will appear to be supportive of us, they may also resent what we are achieving.

> **The state of being in flow is attainable for anyone willing to work the formula.**

Success scares us and we drop back to our comfort zones and what we know best: struggle and worries. Most of us need a big goal or a vision to pull us through this discomfort. Being in flow is the ultimate in harnessing knowledge, discipline, experience and learning. You become focused, energised and aligned with your goals and budgets. In flow, you are capable of big results.

The path to being in flow
The opposite of being in flow is mechanics. Mechanics is where salespeople hate to be, doing what most sales managers call the numbers

game: following the systems, the cold calls, the routine, detail, paperwork, planning. Managers don't realise that when they try to pull their people back to the basics, whether through a course or a workshop, what they are trying to do is to get their people into mechanics.

This type of work is not appealing to most salespeople. They want to get out there in front of a client. They are people- oriented. They are driven by what makes them feel good and that's being around people. If they wanted to be around numbers, they would have become an accountant! But, ironically, mechanics is the path to being in flow.

To salespeople mechanics is drudgery, a plodding type of work, boring and seemingly unproductive. They are aware that this type of work needs to be done, but they do it when they absolutely have to, not before. They'll cold call when the pipeline has dried up and it looks as if they're not going to make budget. They'll do their paperwork when the accounts department refuses to process their work, thus holding up their commission. They'll plan when they get into such a mess that they're running late for all appointments, if not actually double-booking themselves and losing important files or papers. Then they'll do the basics until they feel they're back on track again. Unfortunately, to many sales managers' intense frustration, the basics then go out the window and you know that they'll be back to square one in a couple of months.

You can help your salespeople move into flow if they can:

- understand that doing mechanics doesn't feel good to them
- accept that feeling and not fight it.

Knowing they are going to feel that mechanics is drudgery and accepting that feeling is the breakthrough.

Knowing they are going to feel that mechanics is drudgery and accepting that feeling is the breakthrough.

No amount of logic will convince salespeople to do mechanics consistently. They are people-oriented; if they don't feel good about something, they won't do it. They don't like mechanics. You can tell them that sales is a numbers game, that cold calling and planning are the only ways in which they can make it, and they'll know you're right and give it a try, for a while. When the feelings of boredom and frustration reach their tolerance level, they'll not be able to motivate themselves to persist. They'll need a fix of people contact and will drop what they're doing, regard- less of how important it is to their future, to speak to or visit a client. Their people skills are what makes them so successful, their biggest strength. Unfortunately, this becomes their biggest weakness and is the reason they are not as successful as they have the potential to be.

They need a goal or vision to pull them through the boredom and stay doing the mechanics. If they understand the concept of mechanics, know that it's not going to feel good staying in mechanics, but agree to live with it for a while, you will have turned the corner in creating a consistently successful performer. Don't underestimate how difficult it is for people oriented people to do work that they can only do by conscious discipline. Most good salespeople are in flow when they're with a client. They know how good it feels. They won't give this up easily for the heavy, dull, boring feeling of being in mechanics. So, instead, they will try to take the short-cut, the trap of the euphoric.

> **Most good salespeople are in flow when they're with a client.**

The trap of the euphoric

Because salespeople want to have the feeling of flow, they can often get side-tracked into the euphoric. The euphoric is a feeling of exaggerated elation. It feels the same as flow with one major difference — there are no results. In flow, someone is capable of big results. In the euphoric, which feels the same as flow, there are no results. The trap of the euphoric is that salespeople always judge how they're doing by how they feel about it.

> **The trap of the euphoric is that salespeople always judge how they're doing by how they feel about it.**

For example, imagine that one of your salespeople made a large sale early in the month. She felt great and cruised for the rest of the month. It came as a huge shock to her to discover that she hadn't made budget; she felt she was doing so well. One of your other salespeople lost a big client last month and felt the carpet had been pulled out from under him. He knew he was going to have to knuckle under and work hard to replace that client because it was a large percentage of his revenue. He felt flat but determined, and quietly worked hard all month with no highs, just hard work. It also came as a shock to him to discover how much he exceeded his budget.

It is essential in sales and in business to have a good handle on the bottom line. It's the bottom line that tells you how well you're doing. How you feel about how you're doing has nothing to do with the reality. I've seen successful businesses go under because they were managed by people who felt great about how the business was going. Fine, feel good about it, but only if the figures back you up!

> **It's the bottom line that tells you how well you're doing. How you feel about how you're doing has nothing to do with the reality.**

If your salespeople feel lousy about what they're doing (mechanics), and have no commitment to stay there, they'll feel as if they're not doing well and will have an overwhelming impulse to change that feeling. They will do this by moving into the euphoric.

The euphoric has some easily recognised problems associated with it. The desire for the feeling of elation will be very strong.

To stay that way, salespeople have to overlook or not confront any signs that may indicate things aren't going as well as they would like them to. There will be no attention to detail, just an overwhelming feeling of elation.

That's why people in the euphoric are so hard to manage. They feel great about the things that are in the pipeline or are just about to happen, and you can't get them to see that they've got a problem: they're not going to meet budget. How do you turn around people who won't believe they've got a problem in the first place? If you are a sales manager, you'll know exactly what I'm talking about. To demonstrate how strong the euphoric can be, I have coached people out of the euphoric who haven't achieved budget for more than four months and still feel as if they are doing well and are just on the brink of making it.

Take Caroline, a bright, bubbly salesperson who is very motivating to be around. She's energetic, fun and really looks after her clients. They love having her around, and she has a lively social life through her clients' company functions. She achieves budget most months, and occasionally she absolutely outdoes herself and shoots for the moon. Her manager knows Caroline could achieve much better results than she does if only she would stay focused. Her paperwork is shocking and she is hopelessly disorganised.

Caroline spends a lot of her time in the euphoric. When you ask her how she's doing, she will always reassure you that she's going really well. Even on the months where she has a poor result, she'll have some deal in the wings that is going to blow her budget out the window. And she'll be totally believable because she believes it herself implicitly.

Unfortunately, because she's in the euphoric, she will not look at details; she will not anticipate or confront what might go wrong. She will rationalise this to herself by saying she's avoiding thinking negatively. And in her feeling of exaggerated elation, she's not going to allow any negative thoughts to contaminate the magic she hopes is going to happen.

I spoke to Caroline just after she learnt she wasn't going to get a deal she had been convinced was sewn up.

'I can't understand it. He was going to go ahead with it on Friday.'

Suddenly her face lights up as she identifies someone to blame. 'I bet that miserable partner of his changed his mind over the weekend!'

'But Caroline,' I reminded her, 'if he had made up his mind, how could his partner have changed it?'

'What do you mean?'

'Well, if he was totally convinced that he should go ahead, what kind of argument would his partner have presented him with to convince him to change his mind?'

'Oh, he would have given in to keep the peace. His partner is a real bean counter,' (note the scorn of the euphoric for the mechanics) 'and it would have just become all too hard.'

'But you said that he was convinced on Friday, why didn't he sign the contract for you on the Friday?'

'Well, he was going to. He was working on his budget over the weekend and said he would phone me first thing Monday morning.'

'So how did you feel on Friday?'

'Over the moon. I had really looked after the guy, put together all the figures, I did a really good presentation and used the statistics to back me up. There was almost nothing left to decide. And he said he liked it. It was just that he had to finalise these figures over the weekend.'

'So there was nothing to indicate that he wasn't going to go ahead with it?'

'No, he was really enthusiastic.'

'What about the fact that he didn't sign the contract?'

'Well, at the time, that just seemed a formality.'

'What do you think now?'

'Maybe it wasn't. Maybe he was just being nice to me. I mean, he didn't phone me on the Monday morning or return my calls all week.' She's looking really dejected now. 'After all the work I did for him.'

'Knowing what you know now, what would you have asked him when he said he needed the weekend to finalise the figures?'

'I guess I'd ask him is there anything that would stop him going ahead with the contract,' she says thoughtfully. 'But we had such a good relationship, I didn't want to be negative or put thoughts in his head!'

'But those thoughts must have already been there if he didn't sign on the spot. And the bottom line is that you didn't have a relationship. You made a presentation and he decided not to go with it. If you'd had a relationship with him, you would have had the courage to ask what doubts he had. Not just ignore the fact that he has just told you that there may be a problem here.'

So, looking back on it, Caroline is beginning to see what she missed. But at the time, the euphoric will not confront reality. Clients will give some clear signs that they are not going to buy, but salespeople, while in the euphoric, will look the other way or skim over the subject they suspect is the problem.

How do you tell if you're in euphoric or in flow? The euphoric feels like flow but has no results. Flow is capable of big results.

It takes a very focused sales manager to pull people out of the euphoric because they believe that their exuberance is the reason for their success. They completely take for granted their skills, their experience, their knowledge of their product and, most of all, they overlook their intense desire to look after their clients. They are aware only of the bright, bubbly, energetic part of their personality, which is what most people comment on.

Pulling out of the euphoric

There's an extra barrier for Caroline, if she wants to work at staying out of the euphoric, and that is the team she works with.   It's fun working around a person who is in the euphoric. They are energetic, fun and lively; they lift what may be a dull day. If Caroline holds herself in the mechanics, everyone around her will miss the bubble and energy. She'll get comments like, 'Where's your big smile?' 'Are you having a bad day?' 'Brighten up!' Even people who know what she's trying to do will find it difficult not to comment on Caroline's quiet focus. After all, it's her bubble and zest that keeps them smiling and energised during the long days. If that zest is suddenly missing, rather than find their own way of energising themselves, it will be much easier to nudge Caroline into putting it out for them again. Then they can just sit back and soak it up.

I remember when I was coached out of the euphoric, I felt flat and passionless. Before this coaching, I would boogie down the freeway singing at the top of my voice, my tapes blaring as I relived the sixties and seventies hits. After the coaching, it felt to me as if I was now listening to my music with just my head. It didn't move me anymore; it didn't make my blood throb, my heart sing. My coach persuaded me to hang in there for three weeks and those three weeks felt like a totally flat line. There were no highs, just a constant flat nothing. It didn't matter that there were no lows, it felt boring and utterly predictable. I felt as if I should just retire and become a clerk.

The other consequence for me was that my workmates, even though they knew I was being coached out of the euphoric, kept asking me if I was all right. Why was I being so serious? Was there anything the matter? Where was my smile? Now if this was the response from a team who knew exactly what was going on, imagine the pressure from a team who doesn't know what you're up to and wants that energy back again. The whole team has to be alerted to what you are both trying to do.

And what happened to me after three weeks of agreeing to stay out of the euphoric? My results didn't simply double or treble, I increased my results by almost four times. No one could have been more shocked than me. Did that mean that I was going to be stuck in boring mechanics for the rest of my life? What a dreadful thought! Interestingly enough, the small jobs that I had avoided in the past had now become a part of my normal working day and, not only did I not resent them anymore but I almost enjoyed doing them.

There was one other consequence for me of moving out of the euphoric. I saw people differently. I had had a history of taking a strong liking to people, becoming very friendly with them and suddenly a few months later, finding that they changed. At least, that was how it seemed to me. The changed person seemed quite different from the person I had known, and I would back off, surprised and disconcerted. What had really happened was that the euphoric was so strong that I had ignored the signs of what was really happening. After coming out of the euphoric, I saw people for what they were, right from the beginning. There were no surprises further down the track. Because I saw the complete person from the beginning, I was able to accept them. When the less appealing side of them appeared, I was more than ready to handle it. Previously, I would have interpreted seeing the less- appealing side as being negative and would have rejected it out of hand.

It also takes enormous amounts of energy to stay in the euphoric, keeping your clients and all the people you work with high on energy. People in the euphoric will have regular flat days where they feel the need to recharge. They will feel restless and unable to concentrate. They won't even try to push themselves to attempt to work. They'll judge how they are doing by how they feel, and they feel flat. This means that they think they need to do something to recharge. The idea of settling down and losing themselves in work will not occur to them because, in their opinion, that will only increase the flat feeling. They'll waste these days in catching up with people they like so they can recharge or by talking someone in the office into going out to lunch for the afternoon.

Flow doesn't have this energy drain. Once people come out of the euphoric, they'll find their moods and energy become more level. There will be fewer highs and fewer lows. While it will feel flat to them, their families will probably be happy with the change and they'll start to become more effective. But first you've got to get them to agree to stay out of the euphoric and accept the flat feeling for a few weeks.

You will need to do two things. Firstly, find a goal, through the laws of real value, that they want to achieve very badly. This will help pull them through the feeling of drudgery. Secondly, prepare the people around them to be supportive of them. You will need to have frequent meetings with them and check that they are on track. You may have to remind them of their goal. Coming out of the euphoric is a flat, unpleasant feeling for a salesperson.

Salespeople associate flat feelings with failure. It is very uncomfortable for them to stay in this state. They will feel passionless, possibly for several weeks. This is a difficult state to remain in for someone whose normal day consists of at least a couple of highs. So the motivation to change must remain strong, reinforced by both you and the people you are coaching. Meet with them every week, even twice a week if necessary, and listen to how they feel. How they feel is going to be the most important thing to them. Even when they start to get results they will still doubt that the success is coming from anything they are doing. How can they be so successful if they feel so flat? Stay with them and you'll gain salespeople who achieve their full potential. And after all, isn't that the whole point of your job?

> **Salespeople associate flat feelings with failure. It is very uncomfortable for them to stay in this state.**

Occasional duck to consistent eagle

A salesperson I worked with had the reputation of being the best in the company — most of the time. Mario would have months where he achieved 150 per cent of budget. But then he would drop to 75 per cent of budget for the following months. The sales manager thought that maybe what he did was put so much work through in his successful months that he would spend the following months catching up with all the paperwork and bits and pieces associated with getting the business through the system. While I didn't think this was the case with this person, the amount of paperwork that the reps have to do is something the sales manager should examine regularly to see where it can be reduced.

This salesperson's performance was so inconsistent that, at the end of the year, a mediocre but consistent rep in his team made it to top rep. Mario was horrified. He'd been beaten by someone who had a fraction of his ability, and he became determined to get more consistent results. His manager asked me to work with him.

Mario was a very ambitious person and was strongly self-motivated. But after his over-achieving month, I noticed that he became very disorganised. In fact, I could see it coming on before the end of the successful month. I could see in his day-to-day work that he was getting frustrated as he lost the occasional file or ran late for the odd appointment. He started writing notes and taking messages on pieces of paper instead of writing them in his diary, and then he would lose the pieces of paper. There was quite a noticeable difference in his behaviour in the successful months and in the below-budget months. So we went to work on it together.

I explained to him the formula for peak performance. He strongly associated with flow. This was the miraculous state he was in when he over-achieved. It was wonderful and seemed almost effortless, even though he was extremely busy. It was when he was out of flow that everything seemed hard work and frustrating.

I realised that he had dropped from flow, down past mechanics to what I call the sabotage level. Our fear of success is extremely strong, far stronger than our fear of failure. After all, if you fail at something, you usually have a support group rallying to your side to support you. There is usually a core of family and friends who stand by you and feel good about being able to support you when you're down. But when you succeed, you risk the friendships you value, and the family support. People's insecurities show when someone around them has been very successful. When you are successful, you may gain everything you have always wanted, but you may lose everything you already have.

When you are successful, you may gain everything you have always wanted, but you may lose everything you already have.

Sabotage reinforces the belief that you are only allowed success in very small doses. At this level, there is lots of drama, systems fall apart and you become unhappy and frustrated. You don't know what it is that you are doing differently. You only know that everything is different.

I discovered that Mario's family envied his success, so he had lots of subconscious messages to not be so good, or to be good for only short periods of time. He then fell into sabotage, destroying his success by becoming disorganised and having to work really hard to try and get back up again. We worked on moving from sabotage to consciously staying in mechanics. He would consciously organise his day, slow down from the frantic pace he normally worked at and ensure he was absolutely thorough in everything he did. Slowly the frustration, unhappiness and critical self-talk changed and his emotions levelled out. Mario even threw out his desk pad to prevent him from writing notes anywhere but in his diary.

Again, he moved up into flow, but this time he was less driven. As he was consciously aware of the warning signs that would precede his drop out of flow, whenever he identified that he was starting to push too hard, starting to run late for appointments or starting to misplace files, he would slow down and work consciously until he was in flow again. The last I knew, Mario had been consistently achieving 120 per cent of budget for six months. He is less stressed and more consistent. This was one of the most satisfying coaching experiences I've had.

Summary

Being in flow:

- gives consistently big results
- looks easy
- follows proven systems and methods religiously, but still is spontaneous and follows gut feeling
- means less anxiety and stress.

Being in euphoric:

- gives inconsistent results
- means being out of touch with reality
- means does not confront
- is compulsive
- requires that no attention be given to detail
- feels like flow, but is an exaggerated feeling of elation
- feels good, so salespeople like to stay in it

- takes lots of energy, and is followed by flat days for recharging
- means missing things that should have been confronted or handled.

Being in mechanics:
- will feel like drudgery, plodding, seemingly unproductive work
- means back to basics, cold calling, planning, paperwork, routine work that doesn't involve people
- feels flat, boring and passionless.
- Staying in mechanics is the only way to get to flow. Knowing that it will feel like drudgery and accepting that feeling, is the breakthrough.

Being in sabotage:
- happens after some success
- means systems fall apart and become disorganised
- feels unpleasant and frustrating
- creates lots of drama, both at work and in the personal life
- reinforces a belief that we are allowed success in very small doses.

10 TEAM BUILDING: DIFFERENCES THAT GET IN THE WAY

When I was the classified advertising manager for two daily newspapers, I had the final say on the legal and moral guidelines for the paper's classified pages. If there was any doubt about any advertisements from the public, I was the bush lawyer who said what they could or could not say. This involved knowing the legal requirements of the *Fair Trading Act*, as well as the moral or ethical attitudes of the management of the paper. And, of course, I had to know ways around all these issues.

I used to have a regular meeting with a businessman whose advertisements, for a reason I will explain in a minute, were always on the edge of what was acceptable. He tried hard to promote his business so he could make it more profitable. And he truly regarded his staff as his greatest resource, a phrase that many companies use but few act on. This chap, however, had plans that ensured his staff were well supported, and he followed them very strictly. One of the reasons we worked together was because there was a downturn in his industry and he was branching out into an area he had little experience in, simply so he didn't have to lay off any of his staff. So we worked together to create advertisements that would work for his business while staying within the guidelines the paper laid down.

Now, I want you to stop and examine for a moment how you feel about this businessman. How would you act towards him if you were to be introduced to him? If you had to work with him? He seems a decent sort of a chap, a hard-working businessman who cares about his staff. This man was a pimp. How do you feel about him now? How would you act now if you met him? If you had to work with him? Stop for a moment and see how your attitude has changed.

Everything I said about him was true. His business had been booming because of an influx of construction workers from around the world in the area, building a huge manufacturing plant. Once the plant was complete, there was a downturn in his business. He turned to running an escort agency so that he could keep his girls in work.

In the first instance, you would have made a judgement about the businessman and you would have behaved a certain way towards him. When you discovered he was a pimp, you would have made another judgement about him and you would act differently towards him. In other words, thoughts lead to attitude which leads to behaviour.

It is important to realise how much we judge people, often without even realising it. I have given an extreme example of someone who is noticeably different in morals, but you are working every day with people who are subtly different from you. The differences within business teams, and the way those differences make it more difficult for the team to achieve together can cause you unnecessary frustration and stress if you don't understand why other people work the way they do.

Wouldn't it be nice if building a team involved getting a group of people together who were all alike, got on well together and understood and agreed with each other? It might save lots of time, trouble and energy, but it's unlikely to be successful. Differences within a team create the friction that can move the team forward. But differences can also cause us many problems.

Carl Jung identified differences in the way in which we function. The mother–daughter scientist team of Myers Briggs developed these theories further. In the business community, these differences can take the focus of a team off the job and put it onto each other. Misunderstanding these differences means that a team puts unnecessary pressure and increased stress on each other and on other departments as a whole.

Understanding differences means that the team can allow for them, even capitalise on them, and work together cooperatively. The focus will be on the job, not on problems with other people. Understanding these differences will mean you will be able to find a way of communicating with your boss that works more effectively than the way you communicate now. You will be able to identify which of these types your clients are, and be able to communicate with them in the way that suits them best. Think of the advantage this will give you, especially with problem clients. Once you understand the different types, it's not difficult to pick which type a person is, and, as I'm only going to explain the ones that create the biggest problems, the differences are not hard to spot. You don't have to do a complex psychological test on them. Just read on, then watch them. It's that easy.

The introvert

Introverts are probably the most misunderstood and disadvantaged people in today's society. As things change more quickly and we get busier, we demand quick thinkers and instant decision-makers who think on their feet. We tend to dismiss anyone who appears not to work this way, is not verbally expressive and appears to be slow in giving feedback. And while introverts may be quick thinkers, their way of working things through means they need to be approached in a different way from extroverts.

Miguel has a preference for introversion that makes him good at thinking things through very thoroughly. Analysing plans and making decisions based on logic and objective considerations are his real strengths. He's a quiet fellow and very private. You won't find him chattering away on Monday morning about what he did during the weekend. In fact, you may have worked with him for several years and probably don't know who his friends are. But you are probably aware that while Miguel has fewer friends than, say, your average extrovert, his friendships run very deep. And it's the same with his interests. He tends to specialise and constantly deepen his knowledge about his chosen subjects. In fact, most of his attention is internally focused on thoughts and concepts. He likes, and needs, to go away and think things through on his own.

Introverts do their best work internally in reflection, not externally in action like the extrovert. A vital aspect to understanding Miguel and how he works at his best is that he prefers to think things through on his own, and will share with other people only when it is clear what conclusions he has come to. He prefers to communicate through reading and writing rather than talking and listening.

> **Introverts do their best work internally in reflection, not externally in action like the extrovert.**

To get the best from Miguel, there are two things to remember. If you want a decision from him at a meeting, give him the information before the meeting so he has time to think about it. He will come to the meeting with his decision made, and quietly announce it. And because he has put a lot of thought into it, he just may come up with some aspects that the extroverts have overlooked.

Often in meetings, Miguel will be very quiet. You may wonder if he's listening or if he's lost the plot. If you believe that he's lost the plot, this attitude will dictate what you think about him and how you behave towards him. Miguel doesn't contribute too much to any discussion and you may be surprised to know that he has similar thoughts to others at a meeting, he just doesn't say them unless he's had time to think them through on his own.

Miguel gets very drained if he's with other people all day. He needs to energise himself by getting away on his own to recharge his batteries. It is surprising to realise that many leading businesspeople, who lead very public lives, have a preference for introversion. Maybe it's the strength of the thinking that gets them to the top, but once there every public appearance is an ordeal, even though they appear to be relaxed and comfortable.

While people may have a natural preference for introversion, they may develop good enough skills from the other end of the scale to appear to others as extroverts. Take Sara, for example. She is single, well liked, and enjoys socialising with people at work and her clients. It's because Sara is well liked that many of her friends would like to see her get a partner to share her life with. So her colleagues constantly condemn and tease her about her weekends and spare time. She spends it all at home with her animals and in her garden.

What her friends haven't realised is that Sara has a strong preference for introversion, even though she appears to be an outgoing extrovert. She desperately needs time at home on her own to recharge after spending so much of her work time with other people. In fact, if Sara's working social life spills over into her weekends too often, she gets ill and is forced to stay home in bed. This, of course, gives her time on her own to recharge. Well-intentioned as her friends are, they make her long for her solitary private life. To her it's deeply satisfying.

The most important thing to remember about introverts is that their strengths are hidden; they are very good at thinking and reflecting. Their weaknesses are in verbal communication and being asked to make decisions on the spot. They will appear hesitant, and may even become physically clumsy in their distress at being forced to make a decision without the opportunity of thinking it through.

If you want to communicate well with introverts, do it in writing. Send them memos asking for suggestions or a decision. You'll receive a written answer with a sound decision after they have thought it through quietly on their own. If you ask for and expect an answer on the spot in a meeting, you're wasting their talents and your time.

The extrovert

Gerry is an extrovert. He is energised by being with others and it shows. He is considered to be a sociable fellow, easy to get to know, and he seems to have the knack of getting on easily with every person he meets. He has lots of friends. Gerry is valued by his company for his quick decisions. You can ask him something out of the blue and he'll think it through out loud until he comes to a decision on the spot. Everyone knows when extroverts are thinking things through because they talk as they do it. Introverts are often critical of the extrovert and this method of thinking. Because introverts never speak until they have made their final decision, people who talk their way through a decision appear to the introvert to be changing their minds. Extroverts will think one way at the start, but may be thinking the opposite once they have discussed all the implications.

To Miguel, it will seem as if Gerry is changing his mind all the time.

Gerry's chatter will drive him to distraction, and he may discount much of what Gerry says because he never knows what he's finally going to decide or what opinion he's going to settle on.   Gerry's strengths are obvious. He's a good people person, an easy communicator and motivating to be around.

Gerry doesn't have to be warned about what will be discussed at a meeting, he'll be quite comfortable being asked to give his opinions and ideas on the spot.

One of Gerry's weaknesses is that his ideas and decisions may not be as well thought out as they could be. Another is that he will tend to undervalue the input of introverts like Miguel. He may assume Miguel is simply not able to keep up and will waste the huge contribution he has to offer. This would be a pity, because Miguel's thinking ability would complement his action-oriented abilities.

Feeling people-oriented people
The main concern of feeling people is the impact things will have on other people. If you decide to rearrange the office, their immediate concern will be how to minimise the impact on the staff. These are the folk who are good at understanding people and harmony is their total priority.

Feeling people make their decisions according to what they like, rather than using objective considerations or logic. They are not good at hiring staff for this very reason. If they like an applicant they interview they will want to hire that person. They may not even check references. They will find ways to justify why that person should be hired. And because it is their natural inclination to appreciate spontaneously, if a candidate's flaw is pointed out to them, they will be very confident that they can change things — fix it and make it all right.

> **Feeling people make their decisions according to what they like, rather than using objective considerations or logic.**

I'm very familiar with this type of preference because I'm a strong feeling type. This means I'm good with people in training and coaching, but I should never be allowed to interview my own staff without someone screening them for me first. I do a good job of screening candidates for my clients and can be quite firm on whether they should be hired or not, but when I'm interviewing for my company, all my knowledge and experience goes out the window and I pick the person I like. Even my biggest purchasing decisions will be based on whether I like it, regardless of the logic of the purchase. This is why it is important to identify the differences in your team. Would you let some of your major purchasing decisions be made by a feeling person? If the purchase directly involves that person's department, you shouldn't!

If feeling people don't like one of your decisions, no amount of logic will change their mind. Here is a typical scenario.

Roger's company has offered him a promotion, but his wife is having trouble coming to terms with the idea because the promotion would mean moving to another state. Roger is a thinking-logical person and Ayse is a feeling person.

'It's such a great opportunity! If I stay here, it will take another ten years before I get offered the equivalent position. It's virtually a shortcut up the ladder.' Roger is really excited, and convinced that once Ayse understands the impact this move will have on his career she'll be excited too. But Ayse appears hesitant.

'But what about the children's schooling? They're both doing so well. A move is going to totally upset them and disrupt their progress.' Notice her first concern is for what the impact will be on people.

'But with the extra money I'll be getting, we can afford to send them to a private school. Get them tutors if you like.' To Roger, the whole thing is quite simple, but then logic always is.

'That's not the point.'

'Then what is the point? Anyone would think you don't want me to get ahead.'

'It's not that. Of course I do. It's just that it's such a huge disruption.'

In other words, Ayse decides things on the basis of what she likes or doesn't like, because of the impact the decision will have on people, on her values, and especially on her family. Harmony is all important to her and other feeling people. So, she doesn't want to move, no matter how unreasonable it might appear.

Now if you were a feeling person, imagine the difficulty you would have in trying to explain how you made your decision to a thinking-logical person. Thinking people make their decisions based on logic and objective considerations. They tend to decide things impersonally according to analysis and principles. Emotion and the impact on people never come into the equation. If it's a good move for the business, then it must logically be good for the people.

Now take this into the business arena. Let's imagine that the manager of a department has to reprimand a staff member. Let's see how Vincenzo, a feeling person, handles reprimanding a staff member. He'll consider an aspect of the situation that would never occur to a thinking-logical person, the impact this little talk is going to have on the staff member. So, before he works out what he's going to say, Vincenzo will work out how to present it in a way that won't upset the staff member. Feeling people often water things down a little so that the other person doesn't get upset. The danger is that the other person may not realise the seriousness of the situation. If you ask Vincenzo why he handled it that way, he'll explain that it felt better that way — after all, while you do have to enforce the company standards, you don't need to upset staff in the process.

> **Feeling people often water things down a little so that the other person doesn't get upset.**

If Vincenzo has to persuade Frances, a thinking-logical person, to do something differently, talking about the impact on other people, which is what he would instinctively do, will not work.

Vincenzo's decision-making pattern

Vincenzo must try and put it in as logical a frame as possible. If it's logical and makes sense to Frances, she'll understand and will cooperate. But if she doesn't understand and it doesn't make sense, she'll continue to do things her way.

Vincenzo persuades with emotion; Frances will only relate to reasoning. Vincenzo will find it hard to explain in logical terms why he made the decisions he did because he simply liked the idea and went with it, or he didn't like the idea and opposed it.

Thinking-logical people

Thinking-logical people make their decisions on objective considerations and logic. Frances will think about a problem, this will dictate her attitude to it, which will dictate her behaviour. How she feels about a problem is not part of her decision-making process.

> **Thinking-logical people make their decisions on objective considerations and logic.**

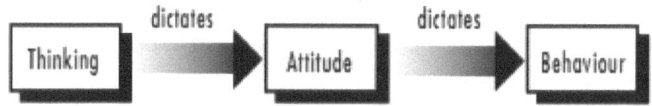

Frances's decision-making pattern

Frances will handle reprimanding an employee in a straightforward and uncomplicated manner. She will simply point out the problem, explain the consequences of doing things incorrectly and reconfirm the desired behaviour. She will walk away satisfied that she has addressed the problem. What she may miss is the reason that person had a problem doing the job in the first place. Because Frances focuses only on the task, she may overlook some of the emotional issues for that person around the job. In fact, if she suspects there is still a problem, she may go back and focus even more strongly on the tasks involved. What she may be overlooking is the person who is doing the tasks and the emotions that person may be feeling about the tasks. One day her staff member will spit the dummy and she will have had no idea that there was anything wrong that hadn't been dealt with. I have seen this happen often, especially with managers with a technical background.

Thinking-logical people will miss the signs and body language of people around them. They may not notice tension in a department and will not notice low morale unless someone points it out to them, in a logical manner of course. And even then, because they overlook the impact of events on people, they will expect it to pass. After all, they're all there just to get the job done, not to party.

> **Thinking-logical people will miss the signs and body language of people around them.**

I saw a perfect example of how these two types misunderstand each other and don't communicate properly. Two women were working in an office together: Carina was a feeling type and Jenny was a thinking-logical type. Carina was very aware that a small faction in the office was creating problems and stirring up several other people in the department. She believed that Jenny should know about it as Jenny was the supervisor of those causing the problem. Carina approached Jenny and explained that she would like to talk to her 'when she had a minute'. Notice that Carina didn't want to alarm Jenny, so she watered down the importance of the discussion. Jenny on the other hand, was busy. She asked if they could talk later, once she'd got her report finished. Carina agreed and went back to her office.

Later that day, when Jenny had finished the report, she realised that she had board papers to attend to. She remembered Carina's request for a talk, but seeing that she hadn't returned to remind her or insist on the meeting, Jenny decided that it couldn't be that important and carried on with her work. Carina decided that Jenny was simply not interested and so didn't pursue the subject further.

Carina is a feeling person and she is now working in an environment where there is a negative impact on the people in the office from the two troublemakers. As far as she can see, Jenny doesn't seem to notice or care and Carina cannot work in an atmosphere where people aren't cared for. Suddenly, Jenny has two problems explode at once. The troublemakers go too far and all hell breaks loose, and when she goes to Carina for support and to try to find out what is going on she finds that Carina herself is on the point of resigning.

Even when there isn't trouble brewing, Carina doesn't feel Jenny appreciates her. It seems to her that Jenny is always picking holes in any plans that Carina puts forward. Carina sees herself as a caring, nurturing person, and feels that Jenny is cold, doesn't care about Carina or any of the staff, and is a critical person.

If Carina and Jenny could understand their differences, they would work very well together as a team. Carina needs to understand that Jenny's strengths are logic and analysis. This is why she spontaneously criticises or finds the weak link in any logic. Carina could be Jenny's ears and eyes as far as staff matters go, but she has to remember not to water down her messages to Jenny.

Jenny needs to remember that the intangibles have a huge impact on some people, something that she herself doesn't notice. She needs to watch people more and take notice of the little signs that signify trouble.

Thinking-logical people and feeling people can communicate if they are aware of how the other operates. One communicates through logic or thinking; the other communicates through emotion. Emotion has very little place in the decision-making of thinking people. Thinking has very little place in the decision-making of feeling people.

> **Thinking-logical people and feeling people can communicate if they are aware of how the other operates. One communicates through logic or thinking; the other communicates through emotion.**

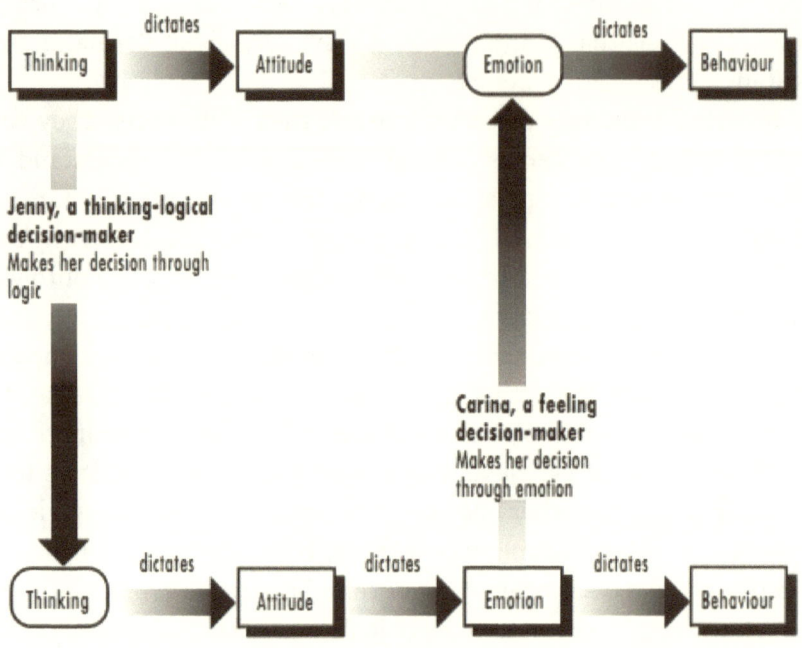

Communication between thinking-logical decision-makers and feeling decision-makers

Understanding each other means that each can communicate in a way that will be effective with the other. If Carina tells Jenny that there is trouble brewing in the office and it will disrupt the workflow eventually, of course Jenny will be disturbed and of course she will care. She wants the work to get done. If all she knows is that someone is unhappy, she won't get involved, but she will be concerned about the workflow.

If Carina understands that Jenny has a flair for making plans work, rather than just seeing her as critical, she will realise that she has someone she can run things past before she finalises her plans.

If Jenny wants to convince Carina of doing something, she needs to talk about the impact it will have on the other staff first, and then present the logical reasons. If Carina thinks the decision will have a positive effect on the staff, she'll like it immediately. Jenny might not even have to present the logic behind the idea.

Usually, we are only critical when we don't understand. These aren't difficult concepts and the different types are not hard to spot. It's easy to slightly modify how you usually present your case. Understanding and modifying can make a huge difference. Other people may not realise what you are doing that is different, they will only know that suddenly you are good to work with. Suddenly the two of you are working well together, getting good results together. Both of you are focused on the job, not on each other. Now you are a team. Isn't it worth it?

Temperament and bosses

When people find out that I help them understand each other, one of the most common reactions is an impassioned plea to help them understand their boss. The logic bosses follow, their ways of handling people, or just their management styles can cause major disruptions to the rest of the company. Employees try to remain loyal but find it hard to understand why a senior manager might behave in a way that consistently disrupts and demotivates their employees.

Once you understand why bosses behave this way, your tolerance increases and you can work out ways by which you can maximise the positives and minimise the negatives (as you see them). Remember that most bosses don't get to where they are by luck. Usually, they have made it because of a series of successful actions in some roles in their careers. It may well be the case now, however, that what were once successful actions are no longer appropriate. They may now be causing problems for their staff.

Some of the concepts already explained in this chapter will help, but there is another concept that my clients have found extremely helpful and enlightening, particularly with bosses. This is David Kiersey's temperament theory. This theory is one of the most helpful insights into people's behaviour and, more importantly, their motivation for behaviour I have come across. Kiersey's theory is that everyone has one of four basic temperaments and that it is your temperament that determines your behaviour. Each temperament has a core need. If this core need is aligned to your role, you are likely to be deeply satisfied with your work. If the core need is in contrast to your job or occupation there will be problems.

The Artisan

The core need of the Artisan is to have freedom to act on impulses and to make an impact. Imagine for a moment that you are at the first footy match of the season. The team runs out and bursts through a paper banner that is strung across the field. This is the image of the Artisan's need to make an impact. You can imagine that sitting in an office writing a report does not allow either freedom to act on an impulse nor does it feel like making an impact. What Artisans will do is leap up in the middle of writing the report and race off into someone's office to pass on a good idea they have had, or to make some enquiries about something that has caught their eye. They won't wait for someone to handle it, they'll want to know what happened, why it happened and what solutions you've come up with. And they'll want to know now. You'll feel the force of them as they come into the office because they are usually excited. They always seem to be rushed and they'll rush you to get the answer.

Artisans are the bosses most likely to be accused of seagull management.

They fly in, flap around, dump on everyone and fly out again. Or they simply fly in, put everyone else in a flap and fly out again. They can be totally disruptive by racing in with a good idea, giving instructions on how to proceed with the idea, then coming back later and changing their minds. By then, of course, some of their staff may have already put hours of work into the idea.

Or they may race into your office and expect you to drop everything to find them an answer to a query. They may interfere, cut corners, stand on people's toes to fix a problem, which if they'd left alone, would have been solved by the right people using the company's normal procedures. But it seems as if they cannot help themselves.

Artisans are action-oriented and become bored easily. Spontaneity is important to them and they are eternal optimists. While they are usually gifted negotiators, they feel restricted by plans and commitments. Anything that stands in the way of them having freedom to act will be avoided, like planning their day and working to the plan. What they don't see or understand is the impact they have on their staff.

Managers of this type need a strong secretary or personal assistant to manage them because their timetables are constantly interrupted by their impulse to suddenly follow-up or share an idea. Running a diary will be a challenge and keeping track of them an even bigger accomplishment. And because it seems always exciting around them, they may charm their assistants into working their way. This would be a major mistake. They need someone to 'manage' them and their time until they can discipline themselves to work in a more structured way.

My experience of dealing with Artisans is that they are easy-going, tolerant and fun, but they drive you nuts as they race in and out of your space in a haphazard way.

The Guardian
The core need of the Guardian is belonging and responsibility. If you have a Guardian running your company, you will at least have stability. These people are the caretakers of the procedures and systems, and tend to conform and perpetuate tradition. They will try to improve what is, and will be vigilant at monitoring and regulating detail and activities. They like structure, rules, operating procedures and other rituals. One characteristic that I find quite noticeable in the Guardian is that, while they hope for the best, they expect the worst. In fact, they can appear to be quite pessimistic. They take duty and responsibility very seriously and expect everyone to play their part.

I recently interviewed a Guardian who was considering moving on. Guardians will often stay too long in a job when it is painfully obvious that it is time to move on. But remember, their core need is for belonging. It is desperately difficult to pull up roots and wander away when your core need is to belong and build structure. The Guardian I spoke to had been with the company less than a year and was returning to the company he had been with before to this position. He said he had never really felt comfortable with them, but couldn't understand why. I could. He was working with an entrepreneurial management team. They would dart off and start new projects, creating systems and procedures as they went, when they remembered. Often in fact, they were just winging it. This made the company very flexible and able to move quickly in response to market needs, but it was a nightmare for a Guardian. They don't like disruption or instability in any form and this can lead to them taking a paternal role with staff. They can also be impressed by degrees and position.

Feeling unsupported or unappreciated can stress a Guardian, as can disrespect and disobedience.

The Idealist

The Idealist looks for meaning and significance in life, and values honesty above all else. You will find these people thriving on a diet of self-improvement books and tapes. They will encourage their staff to participate in all types of training, even training that may seem inappropriate to some of their staff. This type of leader is usually good at developing a vision for the company and communicating it in a motivating way. They will encourage their staff in self-development, even if it means the staff leaving the company to develop further elsewhere.

The Rational

The core needs for the Rational are self-mastery and the acquiring of knowledge. Usually this person likes to associate with experts in their field, admiring and supporting genius and genuine talent. They like to challenge nature and may live a little differently than most. A friend of mine who is a Rational has trained herself to live with four hours of sleep a night, working to her own timetable. They can be great strategists and are only stressed by helplessness or incompetence.

Summary

Introverts:

- like and need to go away and think things through on their own
- will express their opinions and decisions with other people only when they have had a chance to think them through carefully
- prefer to communicate through reading and writing rather

than talking and listening
- are very private people with a few deep friendships
- are energised by being on their own, and become drained and tired if they have to be with people all the time
- have hidden or internal strengths in thinking and reflecting
- are critical of extroverts and see them as noisy, shallow and always changing their minds.

Extroverts:
- have obvious strengths in verbal communication and hand ling people
- are happy to make decisions on the spot, and will think out loud as they make their decisions
- prefer to communicate
- verbally, rather than in writing
- are energised by being with people, and feel drained and tired if they have to spend any length of time on their own
- are very open and have lots of friends and lots of interests.

Feeling people:
- make their decisions according to whether they like or dislike something
- are first concerned for the impact a decision will have on people
- value harmony above all else
- spontaneously appreciate.

Thinking-logical people:
- make their decisions according to logic and analysis
- value reasonableness above all else
- spontaneously criticise or find the weak link in logic
- do not notice emotional issues around them because emotion is not logical or relevant in the business arena.

According to David Kiersey, there are four temperaments:

- the Artisan, whose core needs are to act on impulse and make impact
- the Guardian, whose core needs are for belonging and responsibility
- the Idealist, whose core needs are for honesty and meaning and significance in life
- the Rational, whose core needs are for self-mastery and the acquiring of knowledge.

All the techniques mentioned in this book need time: time to think the problem through, time to identify the real problem, time to spend with your staff member to ensure you are handling the situation correctly and communicating well. Even delegating correctly takes time: giving instructions, describing the bigger picture, explaining the consequences of what will happen if the job isn't done correctly or on time, checking to see if your staff member can do the job, arranging reporting times. Most of us these days have little enough time to do our jobs without adding anything extra. Or so we think, if we take a short-term point of view. So, while this book is about how to get the results you are looking for from other people, you need to be able to allocate some time to make this happen.

Working with managers whose workload has increased as business becomes increasingly under-resourced, and running a small business myself, I know the suffocating sense of not having enough time and the overwhelming sense of pressure that brings. You start your day hours before the rest of the family, work spills over into the evenings, and weekends become a convenient time to work without interruption. You know that if only you had more time or more help, you would be able to get on top of everything. Until then, everything is on top of you. You will not be able to put the information in this book to good use unless you find time in your day to allocate to managing your people better. So, here are some hints.

Decision-making skills

Among the many things that may eat up your time is your style of decision-making. Most decisions come under one of three headings: buying yourself some time, living with the problem, and solving the problem for good.

Buying yourself some time is the easiest type of decision to make. You don't have to look the decision and the people in the face and handle them. This method is supposed to give you time to think about it; time to find a way that won't upset people, time to find the path of least resistance, of least hassle, of least confrontation. If you can buy yourself time, you hope that you will find a better solution later. Or, even better, the problem might solve itself.

This type of decision-making uses up incredible amounts of time. Not only is there the initial contact, but, when you do get around to confronting the issues, the situation has got worse and, probably, the number of people involved has increased. The consequences are then more severe, and it takes much more time to fully address the whole situation with its full set of consequences.

Yolanda is the manager of a department that has installed a new computing system for monitoring stock. There have been lots of grumbles and disbelief that this system is going to do the job it needs, but as it is being installed nationally no one with doubts can object. Yolanda is walking down the corridor one day, on her way out to see a client, when she is stopped by Ralph in accounts.

'Yolanda, we need to talk about the system. I think we've got problems.'

'Ralph, there are always problems with a new system. I'm on my way out, can we talk about this later?'

Ralph knows a brush-off when he sees one. 'When?'

'Look,' Yolanda stops, puts down her briefcase, and asks, 'What exactly is the problem?'

'It seems that stock appears on the new system only after it has been processed. This means that we can't monitor the orders or how long they're taking to process.'

'You're joking! Well, how does this system work for Sydney? I mean, they've been using it for six months. They must have found a way around it. And I seem to remember that there was some report done at the end of the month where you get figures from all categories. Maybe it's in that report. Tell you what, call Sydney and ask them how they've dealt with it. And we've only got a week and a half to the end of the month. Let's wait and see what the report shows us. I can't believe that there isn't capacity in this system for being able to track unprocessed orders. It cost us enough. Okay?' And Yolanda races off to her client appointment. She has just bought herself some time.

At the end of the month, Yolanda has reports to do for the managing director and the board. She finds that the new system does not have the information she requires for her report. It does not monitor unprocessed orders because Sydney, where the trials were done, has a separate system in the warehouse, and the oversight wasn't noticed by Adelaide, which also had the same warehouse system. Yolanda's branch doesn't. And now she has the pressure of the board paper, as well as addressing the system itself. The end of the month means that the other managers are waiting for information so they can do their reports, so Yolanda has to spend time with each of them, calming and reassuring them.

Nothing is free. If you buy time, you pay for it later, with interest. And with extra hassle, extra drama, extra frustration and usually large amounts of extra time. Too much of this type of decision-making will ensure that you are always putting out fires and handling crises that could have been avoided. But, let's face it, it's the easiest decision to make — if you're prepared to put more time into the problems further down the track.

Think of it as the human equivalent to handling each piece of paper only once. You get a memo or a letter and can't be bothered with thinking about it just then, so you put it back in your in-tray. And there it sits for days, rising to the top while we shuffle it around some more. Good time management says, read it and make a decision on it. Handle it and it's done with, gone. Buy time and shuffle it around and your in-tray fills to overflowing with all those pieces of paper. The pressure increases every day with the rising height of your in-tray, until you make a mighty effort and clear it out completely. Or maybe not completely, because there may be still a few things in there that you can't quite decide about yet.

Buying time may seem the easiest way of handling things at the time, but it puts more pressure on you later, and usually at a time when you can least afford the pressure.

The second way of making decisions is to decide to live with the problem. This happens with problems you think you can't solve, or don't want to think about the consequences of attempting to solve. Usually your work will be done less efficiently as you work around the situation. It may seem that you are the only one being affected, but it is a better alternative than the upheaval of trying to handle the situation. Or perhaps you just can't see a way out.

I had a client who used my interviewing skills as part of his appraisal system. I interviewed his people, and found what worked for them and what was causing them problems. I discovered a problem. One person considered this problem a mild inconvenience that she rationalised this way: because she was the only person with the problem, she could live with it rather than take it to her supervisor and create hassles. So she lived with it. Unfortunately, what she didn't know was that there were five other people with the same problem and the same attitude. They were all loyal employees and didn't want to appear to be negative or critical, so, individually, they decided to live with it. Five people being inconvenienced, willingly living with the fact that they were working around a problem that was making them less effective, taking more time to get the job done. When we addressed the problem, we saved five people large chunks of time and we saved the company hundreds of dollars in real terms. If we had put a dollar value on the extra time those five people had spent working around the problem, living with the problem would have been a totally unacceptable solution for all of them.

If you are having to live with a solution, then so are others in the company. It is easy to overlook this. What is the cost of living with the solution? In extra time spent per person in working around it? In frustration and levels of tolerance? In real dollars of inefficiency? It may be acceptable in your eyes for you to live with it, but you need to look at the bigger picture.

I've had managers who have told me that they realise that one of their supervisors is a problem, but were prepared to live with the problem until they had the time to deal with it. But what about the people who report to that supervisor? What about the other supervisors who have to work with that person? They have to live with the problem, too. How much frustration is this causing other people? What other people have to handle the same problem? What other departments? Now start to add it up and see if you are still happy to live with the problem.

The third type of decision-making is to fix the problem for good. This type of decision is the toughest to make. You have to be psychologically tough, you have to be firm rather than a Nice Guy, you have to have a long-term point of view and be prepared to face the possible consequences of short-term unpopularity and resentment. These are not pleasant or easy things to face. Even more intimidating can be what your imagination tells you is going to happen. Remember that emotion and imagination are stronger than thoughts or logic. You have to be strong to make this type of decision, and often most of us think we haven't the energy or resolve to do this continually.

Not every decision is going to need a cut-throat attitude, just a determination to address things once, thoroughly. All that is needed is a long-term point of view that recognises the consequences you may face if you avoid the issue. Don't let your emotion about the possible consequences overrule your decision-making ability.

> **Don't let your emotion about the possible consequences overrule your decision-making ability.**

Practical time management

Most of your days are probably spent running from one problem to another. No sooner have you addressed one issue and go back to your list of things to do, than the next problem raises its head — the boss wants to see you *now*, you have a client on the phone and a staff member is waiting outside your door to see you. You can spend the last half-hour of your day writing a list of things to do for the next day. You can keep a good diary system. But at the end of the day, you look at your list and your diary, and wonder where the time went and why you weren't able to cross more items off your list. So you start again. You transfer things from one list to the next, and the next day is a repeat of the day before.

If you've done any time-management courses, they will have emphasised the difference between urgent and important. Urgent means needing immediate attention. Anything that is urgent is 'in your face'. You're probably thinking that everything in your day is urgent, and you'd be right. But everything may not be urgent for you. The jobs that are urgent for others are the ones that eat up your time. Other people are demanding your attention because the job is urgent for them. And because you get a great deal of satisfaction over handling things for others (most of us do), you drop what you are doing and handle it for them. But was it important to you?

> **Urgent means needing immediate attention. Anything that is urgent is 'in your face'.**

Important means it affects *your* plans and goals. Not anybody else's plans and goals. This, of course, assumes that you have plans and goals. If you don't, then anything with any urgency from anyone will have enough power to distract you from more important issues. Goals keep you on track, keep you focused on the important things rather than being driven by what is urgent to anybody in your company.

> **Important means it affects *your* plans and goals.**

The vital thing to remember is that important things do not loudly demand your attention. Planning, training, relationship-building internally and externally are all things that you have to discipline yourself to find the time to do. They don't shout at you to be done, you have to make them happen. You know without a doubt that if you did these things you would be more successful in your role. They are also all the things that are supposed to be a regular part of a manager's role. If you look at the best managers, you'll realise that they make time for these important tasks because that is what they are supposed to be doing.

What usually happens is that all the things that shout at us to be done come first. You handle them, and then leave the important things for when you have time. Fat chance! Think about it. If people can convince you that their problems are urgent for them, you will drop what you are doing (which may be important to you), and handle them. After all, you're a team player. You support your people; your door is always open for them. And that's one of the reasons why, as a manager, you don't have enough time. You handle every problem that comes through your door, when it comes through your door, regardless of what you are doing at the time. So, how do you support your team and control your time?

Being a good team player
I believe that our growing awareness of what makes a strong team player has become confused with what a manager's role is. Being a good team player and being supportive of your team does not mean that your door is open to every request, regardless of the importance of the request.

Read that sentence again. Being a good team player and being supportive of your team does not mean that your door is open to every request, regardless of the importance of the request. Being an effective manager means that you allocate the time when you will help your people with their requests. If it is urgent for them but not for you and you have other priorities, schedule a time that suits your priorities. If they decide that it is too urgent to wait, they will do one of three things. They will wait until the time you have allocated, which demonstrates that it wasn't as urgent as they believed; they will convince you that it is too urgent to wait and get you to handle it immediately; or they will fail to convince you that it is urgent for you and find someone else to help them with it. This will mean that it is no longer your problem. Once you try this, you will be amazed at how few problems that appear to be urgent truly are.

Take this example. One of your reps has stuffed up her paperwork and she is not going to get her full commission unless you intervene. Believe me, this will be presented to you by the rep as being urgent. It will be 'in your face'! Ask yourself this: can it wait until you have finished the report you are writing? Do you have to drop everything you are doing and handle it now because one of your salespeople has been sloppy and careless with her paperwork? She didn't care about the problems she was causing the accounts department until she thought her commission was at risk. Suddenly, the whole issue became urgent for her. Now, you can see how high a priority this will have for the rep, but is this important to you right at this moment?

I believe that the strong focus we now have on being a good team player accounts largely for many managers not having enough time to do their jobs. We put such a huge emphasis on being a good team player that we don't stop to think what real support is. I'm a strong advocate of strong team players, but it is important to identify what true support is.

Being supportive of your team does not mean that you drop what you are doing because one of your staff has a problem he or she wants to discuss, now. Being a true team player and being supportive of your people may be that you make a time when you will be available. This is teaching them time management, as well as taking control of your own time. Support must be appropriate to the role and the responsibility of the role. Your job as a manager is to make your people more capable. This includes them learning to handle the consequences of their actions. It is easier for people to talk their managers into solving the issue for them than to face the mess they have created. This is not appropriate support on the part of the manager. Being supportive is getting them to take responsibility for their actions or lack of action, not solving it for them so they don't have to face the consequences. This is true support, although it won't feel like it at the time, and some water will have to pass under the bridge before they may thank you for it.

I have found it works if you book activities into your diary the week before — time for administration, time for thinking and planning — and give it the same weight and importance as a client. Let's face it, if clients say they want to see you, you always find time because it is important, it has an impact on your plans and goals. If you book time for administration, thinking and planning the week before, you're not caught in the emotional whirlpool where 'urgent' matters seem to have a higher priority than the activities that are important to your role.

If you can identify whether the urgent matters presented to you are urgent or important for you, and make your decision according to that, you will find yourself gaining control over your workload and your time. If, however, you are racing around frantically trying to handle everything as it arises, you'll never have time to handle your people well, and this means you'll never be an effective manager. If you want to read more about time management and getting control of your life, I recommend Stephen Covey's book, *Seven Habits of Highly Successful People*.

Summary
Handling people well means taking a little more time. Make more time available by improving your decision-making skills.

- Decision-making by buying time costs more time in the long run.
- Decision-making by living with the problem may cause others to have to live with it also, and costs the company time in inefficiencies, as well as real dollar costs.
- Decision-making by fixing it for good is the most time-efficient in the long run and the hardest to do; you need to be psychologically tough, firm rather than a Nice Guy, have a long-term point of view, and be prepared to face short-term unpopularity and resentment.
- Assess every interruption.
- Urgent means it's 'in your face'. But is it urgent to you or is it just urgent to the person who is interrupting you?
- Important means it impacts on *your* plans and goals. Is it important enough for you to drop what you are doing and

handle it?

- Being a supportive manager and a good team player means getting the people who work for you to take responsibility for their actions or lack of action, it doesn't mean solving their problems for them so they don't have to face the consequences.

EPILOGUE

David was feeling pretty satisfied with himself. His team had just exceeded budget for the sixth month in a row and, to top it off, some of them were creating records that were astounding. And, even better, David knew that it was his doing that they kept focused, on target and achieving the unbelievable. Six months ago he had despaired of ever making a difference with them, felt powerless and confused. His eyes dropped to the well-read book on his desk. Now he was as focused and effective as his team. He reviewed the techniques he had used that had made such a difference.

Firstly, David had sat down with each of his reps and had a one-on-one interview with them. And he made sure that this happened at least every month without fail.

Nicole

Nicole was still bright and bubbly and it was a constant project to keep her focused, but it was working. David had covered the laws of real value with her to identify what her goals were and what she wanted to achieve. Then together they had looked at how she could achieve them and what might stop her. It was Nicole who identified that her attitude to paperwork was a stumbling block. She recognised how much extra time it took to go back and fix the things she'd done wrong, the incorrect bookings, the grovelling to the other departments to accommodate her, the sweating and worrying in case she might have let the client down. She felt that if she could get a handle on becoming more organised, she would spend more time in front of the client, and they both knew that when Nicole got in front of a client, she was so good at what she did that most times she made a sale.

David had gone over the formula for peak performance with Nicole and she had been able to see how she popped into the euphoric, and how much she hated being in mechanics. Together, they had made an agreement. Nicole was to stay in mechanics for two weeks. She would plan the following day at the end of the day, which meant that she had no appointments after four o'clock. She would book an hour each day in her diary and take herself off to one of the interview rooms away from the phone and the distraction of the rest of the team, and work on her proposals. And, more importantly, she had asked David to police her. For the first few days, he had checked on her planning and had made sure she was sticking to the timetable she had worked out for herself. Then he had dropped it back to a weekly meeting.

After two weeks, Nicole had been feeling great. She didn't have last-minute proposals hanging over her head, she was getting to meetings on time and her relationships with her clients were improving, although she didn't understand why. But David did. Nicole was becoming trustworthy and reliable, and it was affecting everybody she worked with, including her clients.

After the two weeks, Nicole had celebrated and, when David checked, she had stopped planning and was falling back into old habits. He had sat her down and gone back over what they had agreed. Nicole had refocused and agreed to remain in the mechanics another two weeks. At the end of the first month, Nicole had easily exceeded budget. David had discovered he knew the signs that told him she was getting off track again, and would pull her into a meeting to refocus her. It was working. It had been over six weeks since he'd had to talk to her. She was really focusing on her goals, and it was very clear to her and her friends that she was now capable of achieving everything she had set for herself. She had become self-motivated. David grinned. He wasn't fooling himself that she was nearly enough self-disciplined yet, but she was getting there. The better the results were, the more effort she put into staying in mechanics.

Sonia

David had a one-on-one meeting with Sonia and did the laws of real value with her. He realised he had wasted months offering her incentives that didn't motivate her, bonuses that didn't interest her at all. David was surprised to learn that what Sonia really valued was helping people. She was motivated by looking after them and building supportive relationships with them. This explained why she hated cold calling. In fact, she refused to do it point blank. Once she had clients, they loved her. She pulled out all stops for them in all sorts of ways. She found marriage counsellors for them, tutors for their children, she listened to their problems.

David had demonstrated to Sonia how she had helped her clients' businesses, and how this indirectly helped their families, their customers and their suppliers. He had shown her that when she achieved budget she was taking total responsibility for contributing to the success of her clients. He had convinced her to use achieving her budgets as an indicator of how helpful she was to her clients. If she exceeded budget, her support was beyond all her clients' expectations; if she achieved budget, she was giving her clients good support; but if she missed budget, her support was poor.

Next he had gone over the formula for peak performance with her to list the sort of things she would have to do regularly while she was in mechanics. This had worked for three months, but David strongly suspected that Sonia was in the wrong job. He knew he would have to address this with her over a period of time.

Hamid

David had held a session with Hamid to teach him the laws of real value and how to apply this concept to his clients. He had realised that Hamid took a long time to build rapport. He had explained that in applying this process, the client feels you're really interested in them, you're really listening, and rapport is built very quickly. Therefore, sales happen faster, too.

Hamid had tried it with his next cold call, and had come back jubilant. He told David that his first call was normally five to ten minutes while he introduced himself and dropped off brochures. The next time he came back he would spend a little longer, until at the third visit he felt he could start selling. But when he tried the laws of real value on the client he had called on for the first time, he had been there for an hour. The guy had dragged out his business plan and shown it to Hamid to explain what the new business was going to be about, and to ask his advice! He had even asked Hamid's advice about the competition. Hamid had been amazed at the difference applying the laws of real value made with clients.

Con

David had tried genuine listening with Con. He knew that Con was a Nice Guy and was too soft, but David realised that telling this to Con was going to be a waste of time. He needed Con to tell him. So he had asked Con why he thought he missed some sales and kept addressing the excuses that Con put up. In the end, Con had admitted that he thought maybe sometimes he was a bit too soft and that sometimes maybe some of his clients put him off a bit.

It had been a good start. David had stayed at-the-effect and had asked more questions. What would Con have to do to address this? What might stop him? Together they had walked through the different scenarios where Con felt he had been too soft and discussed the possibilities of ways in which he might have handled things differently.

David had covered the formula for peak performance with Con and he had agreed that when he was with a client he was in the euphoric. David had pointed out that if Con couldn't ask a client why he was hesitating he wasn't risking the relationship, because there wasn't one. He was just being polite and being nice, and his client didn't trust him enough to be honest with him. Con had taken this very seriously because having good relationships was extremely important to him.

Then David had encouraged Con to take a longer-term point of view with his clients, to move his focus away from making them feel good in the meeting, to move from over-promising, and to find how he could help them long-term.

David could see the difference in Con, and his results reflected the improvement, but David knew that this wouldn't be an overnight change. People felt energised by Con in the euphoric and would try to keep him up there with comments about how he was quieter and questions about what was wrong with him. But David was relying on Con putting so much emphasis on relationships that he would keep trying to apply what he had learnt. And he was counting on improved results being an added incentive.

David had ensured that he and Con had a regular weekly meeting where they would analyse Con's client interviews through the week to identify when he had kicked into the euphoric. As his awareness grew, Con found it a little easier to stay in mechanics and become more real with his clients. And David found it easier to keep him on track.

Gina

David had known that it was only a matter of time before he lost Gina to a management position. So he had decided that he might as well give her some management practice to prepare her, and have the benefit of her skills for the department at the same time. He had asked Gina if she would be a mentor for Nicole. Nicole admired and envied Gina's self-discipline and systems, and David felt that it would help keep Nicole focused. Gina said she would be happy to. In fact, it had worked out so well that Gina offered to act as mentor for Sonia as well.

Gina would come and talk to David each week about working with the others and David realised how much valuable management training she was getting. She was picking up people handling skills that David knew would be a valuable addition to her other talents. He wished someone had taken the trouble to train him this early. He was confident that Gina had a very bright future ahead of her. In fact, David started to delegate some of his clients and other work to her. He watched her results to ensure that he wasn't overloading her, but her figures remained steady. It seemed that she could handle more work without stress. Eventually, it got to the stage that, in his absence, Gina ran the team meetings. This was well accepted by the rest of the team. They also accepted her as a natural leader. And David knew that, thanks to him, when she finally did get promoted into management she was going to be well-prepared.

The boss

David now found he had a little more time to think through some of his other problems. He started at the top with his boss. He now understood that his boss had a preference for introversion. This meant that his preferred method of communication was in writing. And, more importantly, he didn't like making decisions on the spot. David had been trying to push his boss into making instant decisions so he could act on them quickly. To David, it made no sense to delay or think about them. As an extrovert, he wanted to make a decision on the spot and couldn't see a problem with anyone else doing this. He could see now what he had been doing, and was almost embarrassed at how much he had taken for granted. David realised that he had assumed that everyone operated in the same way he did. If they were different, he judged them for it and made them wrong. Even worse, he tried to make them work his way. He decided to work more cleverly with everyone.

He started writing memos to his boss with requests for things he wanted to do or decisions he needed. It was suddenly so simple. He wrote the memo, gave his boss time to think, and got a decision. This one simple strategy seemed to change their whole relationship. They talked more. David could see that his boss had avoided him in the past, or fobbed him off to make him go away. He had wanted to take the pressure off not being given the time to think through the decisions. Now his boss seemed more relaxed with him, opened up to him more, listened to him more. David was delighted.

The management team
David put his next strategy into effect. He wrote a memo to his boss describing a series of workshops he was recommending for the management team. These four workshops would explain the differences in the way people communicate with each other, how people think differently and therefore behave differently. Once those differences were understood, people would be able to modify their behaviour to get a better result.

David dropped the memo off on his boss's desk, and made the comment that, if the management team did these workshops, the boss would know how to manage Sam to get better results. They would all be able to communicate with him better. It seemed to be enough of an incentive because the workshops went ahead. One of the results of the workshop was that the team recognised the introverts and knew what to do to bring out the best in them.

After the workshops, the change was noticeable. They got agendas before meetings with the boss, and Sam now came well prepared. David also recognised that Sam had low self-esteem, and adjusted his expectations and behaviour accordingly. Instead of a blockage, Sam became an ally, and the two departments worked together with increased cooperation and communication.

The management team started to move forward with quicker decisions that had been well thought through. Team members communicated better and judged each other less. And David became the one the other managers went to, to talk about their problems. His genuine listening was paying off.

At home

David now knew the difference between listening to men and listening to women. He was a good listener, and now that he was delegating some work to Gina he had more time to spend with his family. He resolved to apply all the skills he'd learnt at work to his family.

He started with his wife, Shelley. He took her out to dinner and had what he thought of as a one-on-one session with her. He listened to her. He didn't give her solutions, he allowed her to express her fears, her worries, her ideas. Her response was all David could have hoped for. He felt they were closer than they had been in years. They talked openly and honestly, and promised each other that they would make a special time each week for each other.

David expected Justin, his fifteen-year-old son, to be the tougher nut to crack as they had not only fallen into a pattern of not communicating, but he could see that they constantly judged and criticised each other. There was a lot of frustration under the bridge and David thought it would be a longer project to reach Justin. And he wasn't wrong.

David found Justin was the hardest person for him not to probe with. It was difficult for him to listen to Justin without judging what he was saying, without kicking into Critical Parent. He realised that he had many years of habit to break with Justin, and he could only think of one way to do it. He asked Justin to come out with him for a cup of coffee. Justin was suspicious, critical and cautious. He'd had these 'friendly' approaches in the past, and it usually ended in him having to give in to what his Dad wanted. David took him to a coffee shop, and spilt the beans on everything he'd been learning. He told Justin about the problems he'd had with his people at work and told him about the concepts he'd learnt, how he'd applied them and the results he'd got.

Then he told Justin about what he'd agreed with Shelley. Then he waited.

Justin's face was lit up. 'Cool! I always thought that you had it together, perfect.'

David cringed at the picture Justin had of him.

And then Justin amazed him further. 'It blows me away that you would tell me this stuff. You know, telling me you didn't know what to do. So, I'm next, huh. What are you going to do with me?'

David was close to tears as he realised his son was not being sarcastic or cynical. He genuinely wanted to know. 'I guess the first step is for me to listen to you and find out what you want. I haven't done that in a long time. I'm sorry.'

'Cool! Anything, right?'

'Yes.'

'Without judging or interrupting?'

'Yes.'

'Without giving me your idea of advice?'

'Yes.'

'No matter what I tell you?'

David felt the stirring of misgivings. What if his son told him things that were unacceptable to him? Hell, he realised that he was still judging by his own point of view. He had to try to see it from his son's point of view, to understand from his son's understanding of things. 'Yes.'

'Well, you'd better get me another coke and you another coffee, we've got a way to go.'

Compared to Justin, Annie was easy. It only took a couple of listening sessions and Annie and David were on the same wavelength. He discovered that they were more similar than he had realised. It didn't take too long and Annie was coming to him for advice. She was serious about her study and education, and David didn't feel so protective of her as he did Justin. This allowed him to stay in Adult with her, and their communication was much more successful as a result.

Summary

David sat back and reviewed how he was going. Apart from the impact the concepts he'd learnt had had on his career, he was feeling happier as a person. He took the time to understand people better and it paid off immensely.

He listened more, told less. Because he understood better, he cared more. But this did not mean that he was becoming softer. On the contrary, he had become uncompromising in achieving the best for people, even when they themselves objected. He had no compunction in handling people firmly because in the long term he knew that it was the only effective way. He became more organised because he delegated more. His decision-making was sounder and fixed problems permanently. He focused on growing his people. He focused on working better with the other managers. He was mortified when he remembered how he used to judge people.

This is how he explained it to Justin. 'I now know that the trouble with people was that I treated them as if they were logical. If they thought or acted differently from me in a way that I couldn't understand, I would judge them and make them wrong. I wanted them to work my way. I wanted them to follow my style of decision-making. I wanted them to communicate the way that I did. And if they didn't, I condemned them. I gave up on them. After all, I can't control the way they behave. Or so I thought.

'What I've discovered is that if I take the time and learn to understand them, I treat them differently. And consequently, they react to me differently. I listen to them and respect the difference between us. And I modify my behaviour to get a better result from them.

'The most amazing discovery of them all is that the more I listen to people, the better I understand them. The better I understand them, the better I handle them. The better I handle them, the better they respond. And the better they respond, the more respect I seem to get from them.

'It all starts with me. How I think leads to my attitude, which leads to how I behave. I have discovered that people's response to me is a direct result of how I handle them. If I want to change the way they respond to me, I just have to change the way I handle them. The answer was in me all along. I only had to learn more about myself and more about them, and understand the differences between us.'

FURTHER READING

Berne, Eric. *What Do You Say After You Say Hello?* Corgi Books, London, 1994.

Berne, Eric. *Games People Play: The Psychology of Human Relationships.* Penguin, Ringwood, Vic., 1964.

Carnegie, Dale. *How to Win Friends and Influence People.* Angus & Robertson, Sydney, 1984.

Covey, Steven. *The Seven Habits of Highly Effective People.* Business Library, Melbourne, 1990.

Goleman, David. *Emotional Intelligence.* Bloomsbury, London, 1996.

Keirsey, David. *Portraits of Temperament.* Prometheus Nemesis Books, Del Mar, Calif., 1987.

Myers, Isobel Briggs. *Gifts Differing: Understanding Personality Type.* Black Publishing, Palo Alto, Calif., 1980.